UNDERSTANDING EDUCATION AND ECONOMICS

Understanding Education and Economics explores the multiple ways in which the field of education and schooling has become closely aligned with economic imperatives and interests, and the impact of this on learning and teaching. In particular, the increasing influence of economic arguments, economic ideologies and government involvement in education have made apparent that there is a need to reflect and talk about economic influences and trends in education.

Drawing on the expertise of educationalists around the world, the book articulates key debates and theoretical perspectives which can give both students and staff across several courses within the study of education a framework for discussing and analysing how economics defines and shapes the nature and purposes of education. The chapters offer discussions and reflections on key issues, including:

- the historical developments that led to the creation of a formal education system in England and Wales;
- the ways in which neoliberalism underpins education, including the coercion of education to serve economic needs;
- the economics of the university as an institution.

Addressing philosophical, sociological, historical, psychological and social issues in education and encouraging readers to pose questions about the nature of education, this book is a valuable resource for students and staff alike and will allow them to broaden perspectives on what education could be for, and what it should be for.

Jessie A. Bustillos Morales is a senior lecturer in Education Studies and course leader of Education and Social Policy at London Metropolitan University, UK.

Sandra Abegglen is a researcher at the University of Calgary, Canada.

The Routledge Education Studies Series

Series Editor: Stephen Ward, Bath Spa University, UK

The **Routledge Education Studies Series** aims to support advanced level study on Education Studies and related degrees by offering in-depth introductions from which students can begin to extend their research and writing in years 2 and 3 of their course. Titles in the series cover a range of classic and up-and-coming topics, developing understanding of key issues through detailed discussion and consideration of conflicting ideas and supporting evidence. With an emphasis on developing critical thinking, allowing students to think for themselves and beyond their own experiences, the titles in the series offer historical, global and comparative perspectives on core issues in education.

Contemporary Issues in Childhood
A Bio-ecological Approach
Zeta Brown and Stephen Ward

International and Comparative Education
Contemporary issues and debates
Brendan Bartram

Psychology and the Study of Education
Critical Perspectives on Developing Theories
Edited by Cathal O'Siochru

Philosophy and the Study of Education
New Perspectives on a Complex Relationship
Edited by Tom Feldges

Sociology for Education Studies
Connecting Theory, Settings and Everyday Experiences
Edited by Catherine A. Simon and Graham Downes

Understanding Education and Economics
Key Debates and Critical Perspectives
Edited by Jessie A. Bustillos Morales and Sandra Abegglen

For more information about this series, please visit www.routledge.com/The-Routledge-Education-Studies-Series/book-series/RESS

UNDERSTANDING EDUCATION AND ECONOMICS

Key Debates and Critical Perspectives

Edited by
Jessie A. Bustillos Morales and
Sandra Abegglen

LONDON AND NEW YORK

First published 2020
by Routledge

4 Park Square, Milton Park, Abingdon, Oxon OX14 4RN
605 Third Avenue, New York, NY 10017

Routledge is an imprint of the Taylor & Francis Group, an informa business

© 2020 selection and editorial matter, Jessie A. Bustillos Morales and Sandra Abegglen; individual chapters, the contributors

The right of Jessie A. Bustillos Morales and Sandra Abegglen to be identified as the authors of the editorial material, and of the authors for their individual chapters, has been asserted in accordance with sections 77 and 78 of the Copyright, Designs and Patents Act 1988.

All rights reserved. No part of this book may be reprinted or reproduced or utilised in any form or by any electronic, mechanical, or other means, now known or hereafter invented, including photocopying and recording, or in any information storage or retrieval system, without permission in writing from the publishers.

Trademark notice: Product or corporate names may be trademarks or registered trademarks, and are used only for identification and explanation without intent to infringe.

British Library Cataloguing-in-Publication Data
A catalogue record for this book is available from the British Library

Library of Congress Cataloging-in-Publication Data
Names: Bustillos Morales, Jessie, 1983– editor. | Abegglen, Sandra, editor.
Title: Understanding education and economics: key debates and critical perspectives / edited by Jessie A. Bustillos Morales and Sandra Abegglen.
Description: Abingdon, Oxon; New York, NY: Routledge, 2020. |
Series: The routledge education studies series |
Includes bibliographical references and index.
Identifiers: LCCN 2019049461 (print) | LCCN 2019049462 (ebook)
Subjects: LCSH: Education–Economic aspects. | Educational planning–Economic aspects.
Classification: LCC LC65 .U64 2020 (print) | LCC LC65 (ebook) | DDC 338.4/737–dc23
LC record available at https://lccn.loc.gov/2019049461
LC ebook record available at https://lccn.loc.gov/2019049462

ISBN: 978-0-367-07465-4 (hbk)
ISBN: 978-0-367-07466-1 (pbk)
ISBN: 978-0-429-02093-3 (ebk)

Typeset in News Gothic
by Newgen Publishing UK

Contents

Acknowledgements	vii
List of contributors	viii
Series editor's preface	xi
List of abbreviations	xiii

1 Introduction: how can we make sense of the influence of economics in education?   1
   JESSIE A. BUSTILLOS MORALES AND SANDRA ABEGGLEN

2 Economics: introducing key concepts and economics education   12
   ROEL GROL, SAM DE MUIJNCK AND ESTHER-MIRJAM SENT

3 Elementary education and child labour: from economic to ecological histories of modern childhood   23
   DAVID BLUNDELL

4 Authority and trust beyond neoliberalism: a critical reflection on education as useful for the economy   37
   ELEONORA PEDRON

5 Illusions of 'choice' in education: shaping the neoliberal subject in the United Kingdom   50
   KELLY POWER

6 An exploration of human capital theory and its effects on the world of education   64
   HALIL BUYRUK

7 Inequalities, precariousness and education: schooling precarious workers   77
   BRIAN MCDONOUGH

8 The economics of the university: knowledge, the market and the state 90
STEPHEN WARD

9 Education as a practice of freedom: negotiating knowledges at a Pakistani women's organisation 104
AREESHA BANGLANI

10 Concluding remarks on the importance of criticality in uncertain times 115
JESSIE A. BUSTILLOS MORALES AND SANDRA ABEGGLEN

Index 119

Acknowledgements

This book has developed out of a series of lectures and seminars given to students as part of a BA programme in Education Studies. The interest in the nature of education and its changing purposes have always been a strong interest of the editors of this book. We are grateful to the British Education Studies Association (BESA) for organising a conference which provided the opportunity to voice some of the views developed in this book. Thanks to all contributors who have made this project possible; their contributions show the dynamism of the field of education. This book presents contributions from early career researchers, pedagogists, educationists and established academics, denoting the interdisciplinarity that makes the field of education boundlessly exciting. It has been extremely interesting to edit a book which seeks to extend the view we have of education and which shows the need for problematising how economics changes its everyday purpose. We would like to include a special note of thanks to Professor Stephen Ward for his support throughout the editing of this book.

Contributors

Sandra Abegglen is a researcher at the University of Calgary (Canada), where she explores Design Studio practice. Sandra has an MSc in Social Research and an MA in Learning and Teaching in Higher Education. She has over eight years' experience as a senior lecturer and programme leader in Education Studies. Her research interests are in peer mentoring, creative learning and teaching, visual narratives, identity and qualitative research methods. She has published widely on emancipatory learning and teaching practice and playful pedagogy. Find her personal website at https://sandra-abegglen.com/.

Areesha Banglani is a feminist, decolonial anthropologist from Pakistan. She is an alumnus of Lahore University of Management Sciences, Pakistan and Utrecht University, The Netherlands. She teaches at the undergraduate level at the Faculty of Arts and Social Sciences at Maastricht University, the Netherlands. Her research interests include informal learning that takes place in all women groups as an alternative to mainstream education practices. Currently, she is researching with members of Pakistani women's social media groups to understand what such network and support entails for their members, focusing especially on the interplay of class.

David Blundell led the Education team at London Metropolitan University until early 2019. Prior to this he had been a primary school teacher and lecturer at London South Bank and Roehampton Universities, as well as community cricket coach and coordinator at Hackney Community College. His work is multi-disciplinary, incorporating historical and sociological material along with insights from children's geographies to encourage critical approaches to understanding schooling, modern childhood, and children's lives. This includes a concern to encourage appropriate educational responses to the global climate emergency along with the multiple challenges presented by the Anthropocene epoch.

Jessie A. Bustillos Morales has been a senior lecturer in Education Studies and course leader of Education and Social Policy at London Metropolitan University for over five years. She currently teaches at undergraduate and postgraduate level, on different education programmes looking at intersections between sociological theory, educational and social policy and contemporary issues in education. An important part of her work is broadening the notion of education beyond schooling, as well as highlighting how education is changed by economic imperatives, and these interests feed into her teaching and academic writing. These interests underpin her editing of this book and her current writing, exploring issues of inequality within the policy of Universal Basic Income to be published in 2020.

Halil Buyruk is a post-doctoral researcher and lecturer in the department of educational administration at Ankara University. He currently teaches at undergraduate level on different teacher education programmes about educational policy and contemporary issues in education. He has published articles on a wide range of educational topics including the education and economy relationship, historical changes in teachers' work in Turkey. His main research interests include the political economy of education, labour process of teaching, social inequalities in education.

Roel Grol has been a senior lecturer in Teacher Education at HAN University of Applied Sciences for over 15 years. He currently trains students who would like to become teachers in economics and business. Roel is also involved in educational programmes that support the professional development of teachers at universities. He specialises in teaching methodology and applied research. His research interests are related to behavioural economics, economic classroom experiments, economic reasoning, transfer, business reasoning, higher-order thinking, and dialogic teaching. Roel publishes in both scientific and practitioner journals and has been writing several books on the education of economics. In 2004, one of his publications won an award for outstanding teaching methodology in economics.

Brian McDonough is course leader of Sociology at Solent University and teaches a number of sociological topics, including social inequalities and applied sociology in the community. His research interests include work, expertise and the use of information and communication technologies in the workplace. He has recently written a book on basic income and is a co-author of *Social Problems in the UK* and has written on precarious work and unemployment in Europe.

Sam de Muijnck is research Master's student of the interdisciplinary program Social Sciences at the University of Amsterdam. Before this, he completed his Bachelor's in International Economics and Policy at Radboud University. In addition to his studies, he is active in the international student movement Rethinking Economics. He was the chair of the Dutch branch of Rethinking Economics and published the report *Thinking Like an Economist?*, which gives a quantitative overview of Dutch economics Bachelor's programmes. Currently, he is writing a book with Joris Tieleman on the future of economics education. His research interests include economics education, economic policy and the history of economic thought.

Eleonora Pedron is a pedagogist and a sociologist living in Trento, Italy. She is part of Diotima, a women's philosophical community founded at the University of Verona in 1983. She works as a freelance pedagogist dealing with training and research in the socio-pedagogical field. She also practises educational support for families, individuals and children, and works as a special educational needs teacher in schools of all levels. Her main interests are women's experience and the educational processes at school. She recently published an article on the role of educators at school and is about to publish a part of her research about the experience of women who have just become mothers.

Kelly Power is a doctoral candidate at King's College London. Her academic work primarily focuses on working-class experiences of education and schooling, past and present, and the ways in which changing understandings of childhood influence educational policy and practice. For her PhD thesis, she is investigating the varied educational experiences of working-class children in the 1860s, before the introduction of educational compulsion. In addition to the history and sociology of childhood and education, she is also interested in literary representations of children and young people in the school story genre, and home education and other alternatives to mainstream schooling.

Esther-Mirjam Sent is professor of Economic Theory and Policy at Radboud University in the Netherlands. Before this, she was affiliated with the University of Notre Dame in the United States and also a visiting fellow at the London School of Economics, Erasmus University Rotterdam, and the Netherlands Institute for Advanced Study in the Humanities and Social Sciences (NIAS). Her research interests include the history and philosophy of economics as well as the economics of science. She obtained her PhD in 1994 at Stanford University in the United States, under the supervision of Nobel Laureate Kenneth Arrow. Her dissertation was awarded the Joseph Dorfman Prize, her first book the Gunnar Myrdal Prize, and her media appearances with multiple Frans Duynstee Awards. She is also a member of the Senate of the Netherlands.

Stephen Ward is Emeritus Professor of Education, Bath Spa University, formerly Dean of the School of Education and subject leader for Education Studies. A founder member of the British Education Studies Association, he has published on the primary curriculum, primary music teaching and Education Studies. His research interests are education policy and university knowledge.

Series editor's preface

Education Studies has become a popular and exciting undergraduate subject in some 50 universities in the United Kingdom. It began in the early 2000s, mainly in the post-1992 universities which had been centres of teacher training, but, gaining academic credibility, the subject is being taken up by post-1992 and Russell Group institutions. In 2004 Routledge published one of the first texts for undergraduates, *Education Studies: A Student's Guide* (Ward, 2004), now in its fourth edition (Simon and Ward, 2020). It comprises a series of chapters introducing key topics in Education Studies and has contributed to the development of the subject. Targeted at students in their second and year of study at undergraduate level and first year of study at postgraduate level and academic staff, the Routledge Education Studies Series offers a sequence of volumes which explore such topics in depth.

Education Studies is concerned with understanding how people develop and learn throughout their lives, the nature of knowledge and critical engagement with ways of knowing. It demands an intellectually rigorous analysis of educational processes and their cultural, social, political and historical contexts. In a time of rapid change across the planet, education is about how we both make and manage such change. Education Studies, therefore, includes perspectives on international education, economic relationships, globalisation, ecological issues and human rights. It deals with beliefs, values and principles in education and the way that they change over time.

It is important to understand that Education Studies is not teacher training or teacher education, although graduates in the subject may well go on to become teachers after a PGCE or school-based training, Education Studies should be regarded as a subject with a variety of career outcomes, or indeed, none: it can be taken as the academic and critical study of education in itself. At the same time, while the theoretical elements of teacher training are continually reduced in PGCE courses and school-based training, undergraduate Education Studies provides a critical analysis for future teachers who, in a rapidly changing world, need so much more than simply the training to deliver a government-defined school curriculum.

Since its inception in the late 1990s there has been continuing discussion about the roles of the so-called 'contributory disciplines' in Education Studies. Some have argued that Psychology, Sociology, Philosophy, History and Economics should form its theoretical basis. Others urge that Education Studies should be seen as a 'discipline' in itself, that the other disciplines should be less prominent and make the study of education too difficult and complex. This book is based on the former assumption that, for a rigorous analysis of education, a grounding in the disciplines is essential: students should have an understanding of the nature of each of the disciplines, be aware of the theoretical issues in the subject and familiar with its methodologies and publications in education. Intended for second- and third-year undergraduates and Master's students, it is the eighth in the Routledge Education Studies series which builds on the introductory guide and looks in depth at Economics in education. It joins books in the series on the disciplines of Psychology, Sociology, Philosophy and History of Education.

The history of Economics in education is interesting. Education Studies began as the theory for teacher training in the Bachelor of Education (BEd) degrees in the 1960s. The Robbins Report (Committee on Higher Education, 1963) recommended the expansion of higher education in Britain and that all teachers should be university graduates. This meant that the colleges training teachers on certificate courses were required to provide BEd degrees validated and awarded by their local university. The universities insisted that the BEd degrees should include substantial theoretical material. Crook (2002) explains how subject disciplines were drawn in to form the academic basis that Psychology, Sociology, Philosophy and Economics were to form the theoretical basis. Economics was subsequently dropped in favour of the History of Education. It is easy to understand that in the 1960a Economics might have been seen as less relevant to education and, indeed, too *difficult* a subject for undergraduates in teacher training. However, since the 1988 Education Act, successive governments have placed neoliberal economics at the heart of education policy, making Economics a critical discipline for serious students of education. This book, one of the first to bring together a series of economic perspectives on education, is essential reading.

Stephen Ward
Bath Spa University

References

Committee on Higher Education (1963) *Robbins Report*. London: HMSO.
Crook, D. (2002) Education studies and teacher education. *British Journal of Education Studies*, 50(1), pp. 55–75.
Ward, S. (ed.) (2004) *Education Studies: A Student's Guide*. Abingdon: Routledge.

British Education Studies Association

Many of the editors and contributors to Education Studies book series are members of the British Education Studies Association (BESA). Formed in 2005, BESA is an academic association providing a network for tutors and students in Education Studies. It holds an annual conference with research papers from staff and students; there are bursaries for students on Education Studies programmes.

The website offers information and news about Education Studies and two journals: *Educationalfutures* and *Transformations*, a journal for student publications. Both are available without charge on the website: https://educationstudies.org.uk/.

Abbreviations

BEd	Bachelor of Education
BESA	British Education Studies Association
CCTV	closed-circuit television
CNAA	Council for National Academic Awards
CV	curriculum vitae
DfE	Department for Education
DfES	Department for Education and Skills
EBacc	English Baccalaureate
EYFS	Early Years Foundation Stage
FE	further education
GCSE	General Certificate of Secondary Education
GNP	gross national product
HCT	Human Capital Theory
HE	higher education
HEFCE	Higher Education Funding Council for England
HMG	Her Majesty's Government
ITP	independent training providers
KEF	Knowledge Exchange Framework
LEA	local education authority
MAT	multi-academy trust
MoNE	Ministry of National Education (Turkey)
NEU	National Education Union
NPM	New Public Management
NSS	National Student Survey
OECD	Organisation for Economic Co-operation and Development
OfFA	Office for Fair Access
OfS	Office for Students
Ofsted	Office for Standards in Education
ONS	Office for National Statistics
RAE	Research Assessment Exercise

REF	Research Excellence Framework
SLC	Student Loans Company
TEF	Teaching Excellence Framework
VC	Vice Chancellor

1 Introduction

How can we make sense of the influence of economics in education?

Jessie A. Bustillos Morales and Sandra Abegglen

Background

The world of economics is very pervasive, and in recent years there have been many changes in the world of education and schooling which have increased the influence of economics in education. This book explores some of the ways in which the field of education and schooling has become closely aligned with economic imperatives and interests. Some of the most significant changes come with the decision that turns the school into a competitive institution that depends on results for survival. This competition has been enabled by the introduction of national testing and assessments, national and international league tables, and the alignment of education to employment demands (West and Bailey, 2013). This means that nowadays education is more than something we take pleasure in and do for our own development. It is also an economic activity.

This book builds on the editors' interest and expertise in education. Discussion with colleagues and attendance at conferences have highlighted the pressuring demands on education, and degrees in education. In particular, the increasing influence of economic arguments, economic ideologies and government involvement in education have made apparent that there is a need to reflect and talk about economical influences and trends in education. Many staff members in education lack a background in economics. Similarly, students attending degrees in education are often not introduced to debates surrounding education from an economic perspective, and thus lack the knowledge to examine how education is intertwined with the needs of economic systems. The editors feel that it is timely to close this gap and to offer a book that engages and offers ways to explore critical debates around economics and how they take shape in education.

The editors have asked other educationists to join them in outlining and articulating their thoughts and their work on the topic. The final product, this book, articulates key debates and theoretical perspectives which can give both students and staff across several courses within the study of education a framework for discussing and analysing how economics impacts on the world of education. Furthermore, the book presents propositions of how aspects of economics are present within education and schooling, and how they may impact learning and teaching. These discussions are not only relevant within the study of education but also in a broader socio-political realm. We are all subject to market trends and demands and thus cannot escape the unforgiving pace of the different economic realities that dominate the world. Knowing more may empower us to act. As John Dewey, the famous American philosopher, psychologist and educator maintained, 'We do not learn from experience … we learn from reflecting on experience' (1933: 78).

Opening up education

Education is a very contested concept, with many competing views on what education is and what is supposed to be for; it is difficult to arrive at a definition (Carr, 2003). As a topic it provokes debate and discussions, and everyone has an opinion, sometimes a very strong opinion, on what education means and what its purpose ought to be. We all seem to know something about education and thus have something to say about education. This might be due to our ongoing participation in education: whether we choose to participate in education or whether we have to participate. For instance, as an individual you might have thought about attending university and you might have considered different courses before eventually making your final choice. However, if you have children and they are of school age, this is less of a choice, rather it is a compulsory activity. Everyone, at least in the Western context, needs to go to school or receive some sort of education, be this through home-schooling or tutoring. Either way, education is an essential part of everyday life, and in current times it is very difficult not to be involved in some sort of educational process, either directly through our own experience or through the lives of others.

Another important distinction to make is that within education there are historical tensions which contribute to its ambiguity. On the one hand, there are philosophical questions regarding education and its meaning, and on the other hand there are more practical questions regarding how, as a society, we see education happening. For instance, we easily equate education to schooling, education as only occurring in schools and other educational institutions, although this does not need to be so. We could think about education as a lifelong process or something that happens in stages depending on our life circumstances, and not just during the traditional school cycle. This chapter argues that there are consequences to how we see education; the very initial steps as to how we define education alter any possible interpretation. For example, if we accept that education can only happen in schools, everything else associated with education is transformed to match the interpretive framework of the school as a social institution. The main relationships are centred around the teachers and the students, the parents and the school, the school and the community. Knowledge emerges as needing to be organised and delivered in the form of a curriculum. Learning becomes something that is confined to the sphere of the school and is quantifiable or measurable through assessments. Students and teachers are quickly categorised as 'good' or 'bad' depending on their adherence to these dynamics. Education becomes subservient to the main characteristics of schooling as a social institution. Schools are seen as places where we must go to learn and acquire knowledge and qualifications which are useful for the future, even if the future is increasingly uncertain.

With regard to education, this book will provide you with 'food for thought', enticing you to open up your ideas about education, to think critically and beyond your own experience and look at education as a system, and not just what your experience might have been like. Whilst drawing on experience is very important to understand things more deeply, to think about education more critically, we need to do more than that. We need to try and take a step back so that we are able to reflect meaningfully. Education is ubiquitous in our lives; in order to think more critically about it we need to make the familiar strange and apply a more sociological understanding. It is very difficult to think critically about something that over many years we have learnt to accept unproblematically. Instead, this book invites you to develop what C.W. Mills (2000: 5) called a 'sociological imagination' within the context of education; a more reflective understanding which recognises the value of thinking about the intersections between personal biographies and history.

The sociological imagination shows us how what we regard as our experience can only be seen as part of a wider set of collective experiences. Pause for a moment and think briefly about your own educational experience. Was it a positive experience? Did you enjoy going to school? What kind of student were you? Would you call yourself an educated person? Why? The answers to these questions might ask that you think about your experience, but in the same way they are what they are because of the environment in which your education happened. For example, if your hairstyle clashes with the expected codes of conduct and behaviours set by your school, you immediately become a 'problem student' who does not comply with school policy. Some people might suggest that you change your hair in a way that conforms to the rules and regulations in your school, but the main issue, the need to conform, will not disappear as it arises from the environment in which you find yourself in. Simply, if the rules on hairstyles were not there, you would not be labelled a problem student at all. Recently, schools have been accused of passing unnecessary punishments to pupils because of hair and uniform transgressions, with some students becoming temporarily and permanently excluded, or put in isolation (Turner, 2018). We might ask questions around why students' uniforms and hairstyles are so important in schools, that we are willing to disrupt a child's education by sending them home if they do not abide by strict dress codes and rules.

Throughout this chapter and throughout the book the notion of education is presented as broad and wide-ranging, with some chapters posing critical questions about education as an extensive process beyond the school and others more focused on education in schools and other educational institutions. The aims of this chapter are to get you to think about education and to introduce a broader understanding of education, from only defining it through our personal experience, to considering how education is constantly influenced by societal changes, one of which includes the importance of maintaining an economic equilibrium or *status quo*. The chapter also provides a purposeful outline of the upcoming chapters, against the backdrop of economics as an added layer of understanding, a layer which is normally neglected when we think about education. Education, in present times, raises questions of cost, value for money, financial benefits and gains, investment, efforts to improve and secure certain outcomes, effectiveness and usefulness. The drive behind these factors is very often defined by what the economy demands at a particular time and within a particular economic system. These factors cannot be ignored and need to be addressed in order to understand how the purposes of education change with each wave of economic change.

This book is primarily written for students, teachers and academics who wish to learn more about education and how the pressing demands of the economy and economic processes seep into its nature and its purpose. Readers will be introduced to various critical stances on how economics co-opts educational processes and becomes a key driver for educational change. The book will use current examples, case studies and theories to explore and illustrate how the study of education could be diversified; that is if we are willing to engage with an analysis of education which encompasses the pressure from wider economic debates.

What is education?

As the key focus of this book is on education, it is important to outline what we mean by it. When trying to define education, the work of British philosopher R.S. Peters is important as he provides perhaps the most systematic framework for understanding education. As Peters' view is very extensive, we will focus on the three criteria which he has formulated; for a full discussion, see Peters' original works (1966; Peters, Woods and Dray, 1973). In his book *Ethics and Education*, Peters provides a 'synthetic sketch' (Beckett, 2011: 239) for the concept of education. Firstly, Peters places education above other important aspects of human learning; he purports education is something that 'is worth-while to those who become committed to it' (1966, 45). That means education is not something to 'tick off' and 'pass through' but something to be enjoyed. In other words, if the learner does not see any purpose or value in the things he or she learns, then, according to Peters, this activity is not worthwhile and thus cannot count as educational. Secondly, 'education must involve knowledge and understanding and some kind of cognitive perspective, which are not inert' (45). This means that education does not, and cannot, consist of the mere acquisition of knowledge and skills. What counts is the transformation that happens. It also implies that individual needs to look beyond their own nose, into other fields and areas; to become educated they need to be able to see the wider world. Thirdly, education 'rules out some procedures of transmission, on the grounds that they lack willingness and voluntariness on the part of the learner' (45). This implies that education is something people 'opt in' and thus the educational process and procedures need to be morally acceptable. This means, teachers cannot 'force' learners to participate in activities that cause harm. According to Peters, any process that does not satisfy these three criteria cannot be called education. Thus, Peters has argued against an instrumentalist view of education, one that sees education as a utilitarian tool to serve society, improve economic and industrial growth and, consequently, the contentment of the populace.

However, Peters is not the only one who has thought deeply about what we might mean by education. Education Studies, as a discipline, explores educational issues and practices by drawing upon a range of theories and methods (Dufour and Curtis, 2011; Whitty and Furlong, 2017). Theorists and researchers in this area might ask why we educate and how. This is underscored by the belief that there is a need to question the nature and purposes of education in order to engage in a discussion about what education is. As Bartlett and Burton (2016) state, you need to turn the subject on its head to think critically about it. This leads them to define education as something that is broader than schooling. They might argue that education is '… essential for human development for both individuals and societies and has the potential to empower, change lives, bring about greater opportunities and enrich those who experience it' (Marshall, 2018: 1). Others go even a step further and argue that in order to accommodate the various 'language-games' and to utilise opportunities, we need definitions that are flexible and open-ended whilst yet being context-specific (Sewell and Newman, 2014).

Depending on the standpoint taken, we could say that people adopt a particular ideology. Ideologies refer to the system of beliefs and values that an individual or a group holds, although some argue that ideologies are something that we as subjects do. For example, Louis Althusser (1976) said that ideologies only exist because they are enacted and performed, and for Althusser education was the most effective institution to reproduce dominant ideology. Either way, it is undeniable that people have different ideas about what education is and what it should be for. Functionalists might argue that education is essential for the continuation of society (and the state) while Liberalists see education as something that offers opportunities for individuals while also teaching us to live together respectfully. It is important to be aware of these different ideological stances because they underpin our views and approaches. In recent years, our belief of what education is (and should be) has increasingly been shaped by economic needs and ideologies, the prevalence of neoliberal economics, and the importance of enabling a market which sees competition as the defining characteristics of human relations.

Education and economics

To explore how economic ideas have become embedded in understandings of education, this book presents a variety of perspectives which illuminate how economics insidiously defines the meaning and purpose of education and schooling. In the past we have argued that education as a subject and as a notion is always under some regime of fast-paced change. We have discussed elsewhere, through the notion of discourse (Foucault, 1987), how education is conceived of and appropriated for purposes other than the pure pursuit of knowledge, self-development or enlightenment (Bustillos and Abegglen, 2018). Discourses 'governs the way that a topic can be meaningfully talked about and reasoned about. It also influences how ideas are put into practice and used to regulate the conduct of others' (Hall, 1997: 44). This book has emerged from such thinking and such reflections. Chapter by chapter, new possibilities are explained to envisage how economics has imposed itself as the prism through which education, its purposes and nature are viewed. Some of the chapters in this book analyse historical and political contexts in which systems of education and schooling have emerged. Other chapters look at more recent events and provide explanations for how education is a plane marked by competition for funding, the deskilling of teachers, the view of students and families as customers, and education as a form of economic investment among others. In this book, the site of the school, perceptions of knowledge, the history of education and the experiences of students and teachers are used to point out and decode some of the discourses deriving from political and economic rhetoric which influence the world of education as a whole. Looking at these discourses is useful because they are a representative of the production of power and as such underscore developments in education both on a global as well as on a personal scale.

In recent years, neoliberal rhetoric and arguments have fuelled an economic-driven discourse about education. These discourses have become embedded in education and have produced coercive entanglements that make it impossible to talk about education without looking at neoliberal ideas and practices. The ways of talking about education as an economic activity have produced an educational reality which we all adhere to. For example, returning to the notion of discourse, there are economic maxims which have trickled down to educational institutions, such as providing good value for money and running cost-effectively. Schools are now asked to conform to the practicalities dictated by these discourses; this means discourses are not just 'talk', what people say about something, but they have 'real' consequences. They influence what we 'do', the actions we take, and through that form the world in which we live. In other words, 'They constitute the "nature" of the body, unconscious and conscious mind and the emotional life of the subjects they seek to govern' (Weedon, 1987: 108). Discourses of this sort are changing the nature of schooling, encouraging schools to think about what their pupils can do for them, rather than what the school can do for its pupils, transforming curricula to 'twenty-first-century skills'. More than ever before, head teachers are 'positioned as managers accountable to the needs and wishes of clients' (Savage, 2017: 143). To add to these tensions, schools are being asked to respond to these pressures at times of economic hardship, years of economic austerity which have left schools very often with limited and depleted funding.

However, this has not just remained an exclusive dynamic for schools and colleges, but is extended to other sectors of education. In the United Kingdom higher education system, the significance of cost-effectiveness and value for money led to the introduction and increment of fees for students and a new form of higher education (HE) league table, produced by a national student feedback exercise, compiled by the National Student Survey (NSS), where students like customers rate and review their degree courses. The results of such surveys are very important to attract students and they organise institutions hierarchically, with those universities at the top of the market producing the best results. Whilst the survey could be seen as a genuine opportunity for students to give feedback, the survey also furthers the marketisation of HE by lodging competition and pitting universities against each other. Interestingly, one of the most prestigious universities in the United Kingdom, Cambridge University, has been excluded from the NSS for two years in a row because of an ongoing student boycott of the survey; students' refusal to complete the survey makes its results invalid (Kiel, 2018). The boycott has been proposed by students and is supported by the Students' Union as a way to combat against the culture of education as a consumable product, and the government's approach to universities This boycott has even been discussed in the House of Lords.

This book is arguing that current understandings and approaches to education are constructed through economic discourse. Market metaphors now dominate the world of education, and schooling has become an essential part of state policy and politics. The development of the 'knowledge economy' (see Powell and Snellman, 2004) has pushed this development even further. As Giroux (2012) states:

> Since the 1970s, we have witnessed the forces of market fundamentalism strip education of its public values, critical content, and civic responsibilities as part of its broader goal of creating subjects wedded to consumerism, risk-free relationships, and the deconstruction of the social state.

This has enabled a discursive formation around 'education for the sake of the economy' (Bustillos and Abegglen, 2018). If we start asking questions as to how we got here, we are bound to find the escalating intervention in education by governments, the disempowering of teachers and educational professionals, the reconstruction of students and families as educational consumers, and the involvement of businesses and big companies with schools, all disguised as raising standards. Whilst it is debatable what exactly this means for learners, teachers, parents and educational institutions, it definitely changes the outlook of what we mean by education. The book is an invitation to think and ask different questions about education, to contemplate it in the light of economic contexts, but also to ponder about the potential of education, what it could be, and not just what it currently is. The question is where this might lead us in the future, respectively, which educational futures are going to be imaginable within this economic logic and how we can help ourselves and others think outside of it.

Thinking about educational futures, Ward (2013: xiii), points out that it is important '... to know what education is, but also what education *could be*, and might be'. Thus this book goes beyond a mere discussion of economics in education and raises questions of the meaning and purpose of education on a broader level. As Arendt (1954) points out, this sort of questioning offers opportunities, particularly in a context where things seem to be in 'crisis'. 'A crisis forces us back to the questions themselves and requires from us either new or old answers, but in any case direct judgments' (Arendt, 1954). This means, in order to avoid a catastrophe and resolve issues we need to make decisions: decisions about what we think of things and how to act. This involves taking risks (Biesta, 2016). These risks seem worth taking as education is about human beings, and hence the book strongly advocates an engagement with educational debates, especially those that surround education and economics. The outcomes of this engagement might not yet be known, but simply closing our eyes is not the solution. '… the acknowledgment that education isn't a mechanism and shouldn't be turned into one – matters' (Biesta, 2016: 4).

Summary and chapter outlines

This chapter has introduced you to a more comprehensive understanding of education and has argued that schools are no longer independent from wider economic realities and government projects. In fact, the chapter implicitly presents education as an essential part of any political sphere and, intrinsically, an economic activity. Year on year, politicians have a lot to say about education, schools are inherently there to serve the public good, but in the last decades education has become the 'best economic policy' (Tony Blair, 2005, cited in Walford, 2013: 7). These extracts in public debate have allowed for a re-imagination of education as a plane where economics is becoming not only increasingly present but also a dominant force. The role of the school in society is changing, yet, it is not changing in a vacuum; instead, it is changing within the shaky realm of everyday economics and politics. Some, like critical pedagogist Henry Giroux (2011: 51), describe these refashioning of schools as 'an attack on education', where 'institutions no longer are designed to benefit all members of the community', but instead are 'designed to serve the narrow interests of individual consumers and national economic policies'. Others might regard this as progress and inevitable in a world where everything needs to translate to economic benefits.

The following chapters continue the debate about education and economics, and introduce readers to the many ways in which the tradition of schooling is being rewritten, not just by changes to educational and social policy but by the idea that education is an economic activity. They offer rigorous analysis of how economics, including its ideological and theoretical stances, is continuously used to define and shape the nature and the purposes of education.

The second chapter presents a historical account of the main influences behind the teaching of economics. It deals with key concepts such as microeconomics, macroeconomics, neoclassical economics and *homo economicus*. This is an important chapter as it explains key concepts and terms which readers of this book are not expected to know or handle already. The chapter sets the scene and explains some of the language which readers will see in later chapters. It also argues that the teaching and understanding of economics is still too dominated by neoclassical economics which creates a 'perfect rationality' characterised by optimising, self-interest and equilibrium. Neoclassical economics is discussed as offering an interesting yet limited representation of human behaviour. Part of the chapter carefully explains how the psychological turn of the twentieth century influenced economics creating another branch of the discipline, called behavioural economics. The chapter gently introduces the reader to basic ideas and definitions in economics, whilst also developing educational implications resulting from how economics is taught in schools and universities.

The third chapter addresses the major historical developments that led to the creation of a formal education system in England and Wales. The developments are carefully explained to denote the increased commitment by governments, to fund and monitor an education system centred around the school as a new social institution. The chapter critically argues what role the formation of the school played in shaping societal beliefs around childhood. An important layer of analysis in the chapter also suggests that the education of children was planned to reflect the economic interests of the time. Focusing on how childhood has been historically linked to the dynamics of school and the pureness of nature, the third chapter uses current examples to problematise the ecological crisis facing us all and the role of the school in educating children about the change needed.

Chapter 4 is the first in a series of chapters which show how neoliberalism underpins the world of education in different ways. It particularly addresses ways in which neoliberal economics coerces education to serve economic needs, and in this process teachers lose power and authority, and knowledge must be useful to have any value at all. The chapter pays close attention to the discourses around *utility* as a way to redefine what is useful knowledge in schools, but the chapter critically unpicks how the usefulness we currently attribute to knowledge is dictated by economic needs. An important argument in this chapter is how educational values of pedagogy, trust in teachers and vocational expertise are being replaced and reinterpreted by the introduction of neoliberal values. These neoliberal values transform the world of education and everyone in it, stripping back the educational experience of many, in order to meet the needs of a growing educational market in which competitiveness and performance thrive.

The fifth chapter continues to use the prevalence of neoliberal values in education to offer a critique of how they impact on individuals. Offering critical commentary on recent policy and educational changes in the United Kingdom, Chapter 5 opens up different ways to examine the effects of neoliberal values in schools. The chapter isolates the notion of *choice* to unravel an analysis of how individuals are made increasingly responsible for their educational futures. Using a Foucauldian conceptual framework, the chapter carefully illustrates how the introduction of *choice* and other educational policies creates an environment which is designed to favour a new type of *educated subject*. The chapter harnesses current changes in educational policy and a Foucauldian theoretical stance to offer a critical account of how the values of neoliberal economics seep into the world of education and schooling.

Other impacts of economic values in education are explored in the sixth chapter. In Chapter 6, *Human Capital Theory* (HCT) is used to shed light on how there is a tendency to think about human beings as investments. Education is also discussed as one of the main ways in which an individual acquires human capital in a world where education success is exchanged for jobs, better pay or to compete in the global employment market. The chapter offers clear definitions of the theoretical stance and a useful historical context to introduce readers to this critical perspective. The chapter narrates how our engagement with education is normally thought about on very economic terms, with education seen as a valuable investment which should allow us to secure certain benefits.

In Chapter 7, the relationship between education and employment laid out in the previous chapter is problematised further. In this chapter, the conflation between education and employment is explored to highlight emerging issues of inequality in the world of work. This chapter delves into the notion of the *Precariat* and the rise of precarious work as a way to problematise the role of education and schooling in reproducing unequal employment realities. The *Precariat* is defined and used to draw educational implications throughout the chapter, raising critical questions about the role of schools in reproducing a workforce facing precarious futures. The chapter also seeks to emphasise the ways employment relations occur in the *gig economy*, a particular climate affecting the world of work and enabling precarious conditions of employment. These points are used to argue that the purpose of education is reduced to that of an *edu-factory*, where the production of qualifications, led by market trends, overlooks more traditional values. Although the chapter refers to UK contexts, the applicability of its critical points are global and can be used to analyse other educational contexts.

Chapter 8 offers critical exploration of how the university as an institution has undergone profound change, and has now come under pressure to renew itself to meet economic demands. The chapter has three main sections, *the mediaeval origins of the university*, *the modern university* and *the postmodern university,* which unpack the development of the institution and the current exposure to changes in the educational markets facing universities. The chapter pays close attention to recent changes in the United Kingdom in relation to tuition fees, student funding and the markets in which degrees are created. In critically discussing these changes, the chapter is arguing that HE has become another economic commodity, turning it into an integral part of political agendas, and incrementally monitored by governments. Further reflections around what happens to knowledge in market relations and the effects of increasing scrutiny on universities are also considered.

The association of neoliberal economics and progress is critiqued in Chapter 9. It argues that an important impact of a neoliberal education is that it is reductionist and Eurocentric. Chapter 9 problematises the development discourse and how it impacts on the projects of schooling in non-Western societies. As part of its analysis, the chapter uses Foucauldian theory to raise critical questions on how Eurocentric knowledge is being replicated in developing countries, legitimised by schools created to mirror the West. These are important arguments, particularly as education has had a long history of being an instrument of colonisation, and recolonisation in developing countries (Brock-Utne, 2002). Engaging in a critique of the belief that any type of education is progress, the chapter also draws on critical pedagogy as a way to decolonise education.

The final chapter, Chapter 10, provides concluding remarks to the book and highlights the importance of criticality when thinking about education. The chapter also contains questions for reflection that encourage readers to explore the topic further. The future of education is uncertain and hence the chapter argues for all readers to engage with education – with an open and inquisitive attitude.

Please note that each of these chapters reflects its author's, or authors', own view(s). Although not all of them agree with each other, they all have a critical, analytical outlook on education and address economics or economic questions of some sort. It is therefore not necessary to read the chapters in the order they are presented, although we, as the editors, have tried to put them in a meaningful sequence, presenting those chapters giving historical insights and addressing more general questions first, and those providing concrete case studies and examples later. Each chapter also poses questions which we recommend readers follow up on, to learn more about particular aspects of a topic or argument.

Conclusion

As explained in this chapter, this book is actively encouraging you as a reader to pose questions about the nature of education and the organisation of important institutions, such as the school. The chapters are a compilation of possible challenges to the dominant views on education. Throughout the book, accepted views on education are outlined and very often questioned to contest hegemonic judgements that prevent us from thinking differently. In the case of education and economics, this book outlines some of the new political rationalities based on 'truths' associated with the economy, the market, human capital and an entrepreneurial vision of the individual (Foucault, 2008: 215). On a more inherent level, this book also seeks to broaden readers' perspectives on what education could be for, and what it should be for.

To conclude this first chapter, we would like to point out that this book is part of an Education Studies series. These books address philosophical, sociological, historical, psychological and social issues in education both on a national and international level. These discussions are equally relevant within the study of education, particularly at a time when within education courses the influences of other disciplines are being made more apparent and pressures on justifying educational outcomes are mounting. We therefore recommend that readers explore educational issues beyond this book and join the debate about education because: education is something that concerns us all.

References

Althusser, L. (1976) *Essays on Ideology*. London: Verso.
Arendt, H. (1954) *The Crisis in Education*. Available at: https://thi.ucsc.edu/wp-content/uploads/2016/09/Arendt-Crisis_In_Education-1954.pdf (Accessed 19 September 2019).
Bartlett, S. and Burton, D. (2016) *Introduction to Education Studies* (4th edition). London: Sage.
Beckett, K.S. (2011) R.S. Peters and the concept of education. *Educational Theory*, 61(3), pp. 239–255.
Biesta, G.J.J. (2016) *The Beautiful Risk of Education*. New York: Routledge.
Brock-Utne, B. (2002) *Whose Education for All?: The Recolonisation of the African Mind*. London: Taylor and Francis.
Bustillos, J. and Abegglen, S. (2018) The co-opting of education: education and education studies from a political and economic discourse. *Educational Futures*, 9(1), pp. 18–33.
Carr, D. (2003) Philosophy and the meaning of education. *Theory and Research in Education*, 1(2), pp. 195–212.
Dewey, J. 1933. *How We Think*. Boston, MA: D.C. Heath.
Dufour, B. and Curtis, W. (eds.) (2011) *Studying Education: An Introduction to the Key Disciplines in Education Studies*. Buckingham: Open University Press.
Foucault, M. (1987) The order of discourse. In R. Young (ed.), *Untying the Text: A Post-Structuralist Reader*. London: Routledge and Kegan Paul.
Foucault, M. (2008) *The Birth of Biopolitics: Lectures at the College de France, 1978–1979*. New York: Palgrave Macmillan.
Giroux, H. (2011) *On Critical Pedagogy: Henry A. Giroux*. Oxford: Continuum.
Giroux, H. (2012, October 8) The disappearance of public intellectuals. *Counterpunch*. Available at: www.counterpunch.org/2012/10/08/the-disappearance-of-public-intellectuals/ (Accessed 12 September 2019).
Hall, S. (1997) The work of representation. In S. Hall (ed.), *Representation: Cultural Representations and Signifying Practices*. London: Sage.
Kiel, M. (2018) Cambridge excluded from National Student Survey for second year in a row. *Varsity*. Available at: www.varsity.co.uk/news/15766 (Accessed 11 September 2019).
Marshall, J. (2018) Introduction: the nature and purpose of education in contemporary society. In J. Marshall (ed.), *Contemporary Debates in Education Studies*. Abingdon: Routledge.
Peters, R.S. (1966) *Ethics and Education*. London: Allen and Unwin.
Peters, R.S., Woods, J. and Dray, W.H. (1973) Aims of education: a conceptual inquiry. In R.S. Peters (ed.), *The Philosophy of Education*. London: Oxford University Press.
Powell, W.W. and Snellman, K. (2004) The knowledge economy. *Annual Review of Sociology*, 30(1), pp. 199–220.
Savage, G. (2017) Neoliberalism, education and curriculum. In B. Gobby and R. Walker (eds.), *Powers of Curriculum: Sociological Perspectives on Education*. London: Oxford University Press.

Sewell, K. and Newman, S. (2014) What is education? In W. Curtis, S. Ward, J. Sharp and L. Hankin (eds.), *Education Studies: An Issue-Based Approach*, London: Sage/Learning Matters.

Turner, C. (2018) Haircut and uniform violations being punished by schools as severely as drugs and weapons, MPs warn. *The Telegraph*. Available at: www.telegraph.co.uk/education/2018/07/24/haircut-uniform-violations-punished-schools-severely-drug-weapons/ (Accessed 22 August 2019).

Walford, G. (2013) *Blair's Educational Legacy?* London: Routledge.

Ward, S. (2013) Introduction: the study of education. In S. Ward (ed.), *A Student's Guide to Education Studies* (3rd edition). Abingdon: Routledge.

Weedon, C. (1987) *Feminist Practice and Poststructuralist Theory* (2nd edition). London: Blackwell.

West, A. and Bailey, E. (2013) The development of the academies programme: 'privatising' school-based education in England 1986–2013. *British Journal of Educational Studies*, 61(2), pp. 137–159.

Whitty, G. and Furlong, J. (eds.) (2017) *Knowledge and the Study of Education: An International Exploration*. Oxford: Symposium Books.

Wright Mills, C. (2000) *The Sociological Imagination*. Oxford: Oxford University Press.

2 Economics
Introducing key concepts and economics education

Roel Grol, Sam de Muijnck and Esther-Mirjam Sent

Introduction

Economics impacts education. But what do we mean by economics when we make this claim? And, to what sort of education are we referring? We are convinced that the economics of education cannot be properly understood without addressing economics education. For that purpose, the present chapter explores economics education in the contexts of both secondary schools and universities. In the first section we summarise the topics with which economists are concerned and the gradual change in dominant approaches that are key to the discipline. Specifically, we contrast the neoclassical with a more behavioural approach to economics. Section 3 illustrates different ways in which economists may look at real-world phenomena such as the level of wages and the distribution of income. Before turning to the education of economics in both secondary education and in universities, we discuss some recent criticism of the discipline of economics. Specific attention is paid to student movements that criticise the economics that is taught at universities. We conclude the chapter with some closing comments, a summary of the highlights, questions for reflection and suggested readings.

Understanding economics

In 1776 Adam Smith published his famous book, *An Inquiry into the Nature and Causes of the Wealth of Nations*. The title of this publication more or less summarises the focus of the early generations of economists: studying the economy and real economic phenomena by looking, amongst others, at the production, distribution, and consumption of goods and services. Over time, the focus of economists has shifted and changed.

Economics has come to focus on human behaviour as 'a relationship between ends and scarce means which have alternative uses' (Robbins, 1935: 15). Today, mainstream economists try to understand economic choices and decisions along with their causes and effects (Angner, 2012; Cartwright, 2011). These choices and decisions may range from someone's personal considerations whether or not to buy a hot dog (Cartwright, 2011), to a nationwide debate on how to respond to a financial crash. The first example deals with economics at a micro level. Microeconomics studies the behaviour of individuals and firms (Schotter, 2003). In a market, supply and demand meet, and prices adjust when supply, demand, or other factors (such as income) change. This is where general concepts such as scarcity come into play. Scarcity refers to the phenomenon that, due to limited resources, someone has to give up something when choosing something else. The second example points towards the macro level at which economics can be studied. Macroeconomists are interested in the (inter)national economy as a whole by looking, amongst others, at economic growth, income (re)distribution, and supply and demand at an aggregated level (e.g., Mankiw and Scarth, 2012). This micro/macro distinction can be found in the educational materials used in economics classes at secondary schools and universities around the globe.

Both pupils in secondary education (Grol et al., 2017) and university students (Tieleman et al., 2018) are generally taught to think like a *neoclassical* economist: 'If you have studied economics but do not know whether or not you were taught in the neoclassical tradition, it is almost certain that you were' (Angner, 2012: 4). Neoclassical economics centralises the idea Colander et al. (2010) refer to as the *holy trinity* of perfect rationality, self-interest, and equilibrium. Firstly, rationality implies that someone is able to optimise his or her choices; secondly, self-interest involves the focus on someone's own benefits only; and thirdly, equilibrium describes either the circumstance in which everything is balanced or the process during which everything balances out. These three characteristics are often represented by *homo economicus*: a self-interested, fully rational human being who calculates faultlessly into optimal choices (e.g., Bruni and Sugden, 2007; Cartwright, 2011). The neoclassical approach to economics can be characterised by the drawing of logical inferences from assumptions, resulting in a resilient belief in the supremacy of markets (Camerer, 1999; Morgan and Rutherford, 1998). As technology advanced in the second half of the twentieth century, complex calculations of the so-called holy trinity could be carried out by computers. The formal economic analyses based on mathematics and econometrics led economists to claim that theirs was the hardest of the social sciences (Wilkinson and Klaes, 2012).

Tugwell (1922) and many others criticised the unrealistic and fairly limited representation of human economic behaviour underlying neoclassical economic theory. However, scholars such as Friedman (1966) argued that, as long as such assumptions in economic models allowed for controllable analyses and generated accurate predictions, their use should not be considered problematic. The latter stance allowed economists to focus on model-based mathematical analyses for many decades, and to disregard, for example, psychological insights on human behaviour (Camerer, 2005; Heukelom, 2014; Sent, 2004).

In the second half of the twentieth century, cognitive psychologists took an interest in the study of human perception and reasoning ability (Angner, 2012; Camerer et al., 2004). Based on insights that arose from this stream in psychology, Herbert Simon aimed at providing economics with 'a fuller picture of economic man' (1959: 279) by incorporating the notion of *bounded rationality*. The latter involves taking the empirically established, limited capacities of people as a starting point for economic theory, instead of the assumptions underlying the *homo economicus* we described earlier (Sent, 2004; Simon, 1959).

A fully rational potential student, for example, would weigh all the costs and benefits of each university and each major (subject of study). She would also consider all the costs and benefits of alternatives to studying. And this would result in a choice that maximises her so-called 'utility'. A boundedly rational potential student would use rules-of-thumb. She would spend some time considering the alternatives, but stop once the choice seems a reasonable one to her. She might select the university and major of someone she trusts to have made a good decision.

Over the years, a variety of insights from cognitive and social psychology advanced the understanding of economic behaviour (Camerer, 1999). A growing body of research from this field of *behavioural economics* indicates that the real behaviour of people often deviates from the behaviour as modelled in neoclassical theory (Engelhardt, 2011; Kahneman, 2003; Tversky and Kahneman, 1974). For example, in the 1970s, Tversky and Kahneman contributed to our understanding that people make use of heuristics, instead of fully rational and perfect calculations. They identified several cognitive biases due to which people tend to make mistakes when using simple rules-of-thumb in economic decisions. The result is likely to be a less optimal choice and outcome compared to what the standard economic model would predict (Tversky and Kahneman, 1974).

To improve our understanding of the mechanisms underlying the choices people make and the decisions they reach, behavioural economists try to work 'constructively with the standard economic model to get a better understanding of economic behaviour' (Cartwright, 2011: 4). That is, existing economic theory is taken as a starting point. By using, amongst others, laboratory experiments, questionnaires, and field observations, behavioural economists try to investigate and identify possible deviations from the standard model (e.g., Angner, 2012; Heukelom, 2011; Santos, 2011; Sent, 2004). The empirical findings may indicate robust anomalies, for which behavioural economists try to find explanations in order to weigh whether or not it is necessary to adjust specific parts of the existing theory (Angner, 2012; Camerer *et al.*, 2004; Sent, 2004; Weber and Camerer, 2006). Following such an approach, behavioural economists try to improve the alignment of economic theory with observations of how people in real life make choices and reach decisions.

Economic perspectives on wages and income

The discipline of economics, as discussed before, is currently dominated by neoclassical economics. Therefore, it often seems as if the neoclassical perspective is *the* economic perspective. This is, however, not the case, as there are many other economic perspectives. In this respect, economics is no different from other social sciences. Take political science, for example. It would make no sense to speak of *the* political perspective, as it is clear that there are many points of view on political manners. The same applies to economic topics. These can be studied from different perspectives that pay attention to different aspects of the same topic, and in doing so all contribute to our understanding of the matter. This does not mean that different perspectives necessarily go hand in hand; two perspectives can be highly contradictory. In such cases, it makes sense to consider empirical investigations in order to decide which perspective explains a phenomenon best. The following example, starting from a bundle of everyday life questions, may illustrate this:

Why do I earn as much as I do?
Why do certain people earn a lot more money than other people?
What determines the level of a person's wage?

The topic of wages has been very prominent within economics for more than a century and there are many theories on the matter. We discuss two basic ones here.

The first is the neoclassical perspective. As discussed earlier, it starts from the assumption of rational individuals operating within markets. Perhaps the core feature of neoclassical economics is the idea of the competitive market. In such a market there is perfect competition, which means that demand and supply meet each other to create the optimal outcome. 'Optimal' is defined as a situation in which nobody could be better off without making someone else worse off. This theoretical and normative framework can be applied to any type of market, including the labour market.

By applying the idea of rational individuals operating in a market for labour, the neoclassical perspective advances the idea that productivity is the crucial factor determining wages. To put it bluntly, this perspective concludes that you get what you deserve. If an advertising executive earns 30 times as much as a teacher, it is because the advertising executive is 30 times as productive as the teacher. The reason that productivity is the crucial factor is that market competition forces employers to consider only monetary aspects. In the words of Thomas Sowell, 'Capitalism knows only one colour: that colour is green; all else is necessarily subservient to it, hence, race, gender and ethnicity cannot be considered within it'. The market does not allow for discrimination and rewards people purely on what they contribute individually. Education, in this neoclassical perspective, is seen as a means to enhance labour productivity. It allows people to acquire human capital, skills, and knowledge, which enable them to produce more market value later on in their lives. People thus invest in education because it will subsequently give them a higher wage, as their productivity will benefit from it (Blair, 2011; Van Staveren, 2014).

The second approach is the feminist perspective. In opposition to the individualistic neoclassical perspective, feminist economics pays a lot more attention to social factors. Instead of assuming that people are, metaphorically speaking, isolated islands that exchange goods and services with each other, feminist economics starts from the idea that human beings are fundamentally social, as economic life is always embedded in social life. As such, social relations are also reflected in economic relations. Prominent among these are gender relations. In this way, men and women are judged based upon not only their individual characteristics, but also their group membership. Applied to the labour market, this means that inequality is not simply a matter of differences in productivity, but also a consequence of discrimination. Following a feminist perspective, the fact that, on average, women earn less than men is not because men are more productive, but because of the unequal social power relations between men and women. In this perspective, employers are not blind for gender or ethnicity and do discriminate based on these, although they mostly do discriminate implicitly. This discrimination happens in hiring, promotion, and remuneration practices and, as such, causes discriminated groups to be employed less, obtain lower positioned jobs, and earn less on average (Van Staveren, 2014).

By no means can we disregard the neoclassical perspective totally, as empirical research does indicate that productivity indeed plays an important role. This is, however, not the full picture, as other empirical research shows that simply being a woman causes one to earn less. Both the neoclassical and the feminist perspectives, thus, provide valuable contributions to our understanding of questions such as 'Why do I earn as much as I do?'.

Crises and criticism

Since the crises that shook economies worldwide during the first decade of the twenty-first century, people from both inside and outside the discipline started to realise that economists had overlooked many relevant dimensions and had overestimated their own usefulness. When meeting scholars from the London School of Economics, the Queen of the United Kingdom questioned whether the authority often bestowed on economists was justified, and wondered, when being confronted with the chaotic state of the global financial markets: 'Why did nobody notice it?' (*Telegraph*, 2008).

Even Alan Greenspan, the former Chairman of the US Federal Reserve Board, and often called *Master of the Universe*, noted in retrospect: 'I have made the error to expect that the self-interest of organizations, especially banks and others, was the best way to protect shareholders, capital, and business' (Greenspan, quoted in De Graaf, 2010: 49). As such, the economic crisis also seems a crisis of neoclassical economics, thus providing an extra impetus to the new research programmes waiting in the wings.

Criticism of economics is not a new phenomenon, however. Before the financial crisis there were similar critiques of economics, mainly voiced by heterodox economists and other social scientists. Frank et al. (1993) suggested: 'With an eye toward both the social good and the well-being of their own students, economists may wish to stress a broader view of human motivation in their teaching' (170–171). This proposition may be the result of the finding in several empirical studies that especially economics students seem to be less likely to contribute to public goods (Marwell and Ames, 1981) and to be less cooperative (Frank et al., 1993) than students in other disciplines. In 2005, Colander asked students to react to the quote 'Economics is the most scientific of the social sciences'. Over 75 per cent of the economics students agreed, which may indicate a perceived high status of economics as a discipline (Fourcade et al., 2015). It may be the case that, by referring to the *holy trinity* mentioned before, studying neoclassical economics makes students more self-centred, or that economics just attracts more selfish students, or (and this is an argument in favour of economics students) that students in disciplines outside economics are not disclosing their inclination to selfishness that openly (Fourcade et al., 2015).

Although an internal debate within an academic discipline about the direction in which it should be heading is hardly unique, a particular phenomenon within economics has emerged over the last decade students at faculties of economics all over the world, ranging from Colombia to Nigeria, Vietnam to Western Europe, have begun organising themselves in an effort to change the discipline (De Muijnck and Sent, 2018). A core argument is that economics education should be more relevant and focus more on current societal challenges and developments such as climate-change, inequality, and financial crises. Another important element of the movement is the call for the opening-up of economic thinking by teaching multiple theoretical approaches, instead of only one. While a few groups were already active before the financial crisis of 2008, the movement has grown enormously since then. Currently, there are over 80 active student groups in roughly 30 countries. The movement operates under different names in different places, such as Post-Autistic Economics, Real World Economics, Post-Crash Economics Society, Network for Pluralist Economics, International Student Initiative for Pluralism in Economics, but the most commonly used name is Rethinking Economics.

Indeed, it is quite remarkable for students to ask for a different kind of economics. In economics jargon, one could describe this situation as one of 'asymmetric information'. The students, by definition of being students, have less information about what is and could be taught than the teachers. Despite this, students have argued that what they are being taught is not sufficient in preparing them for their future roles in society. They emphasise that economists occupy influential positions in society and stress the urgency of addressing current societal challenges, such as financial instability, climate-change, and growing social polarisation. In order to achieve change they organise events, actively campaign to change curricula, educate themselves, and create networks for like-minded students and academics. Interestingly, these calls for change do not seem to have resulted in a major change of economics curricula so far (Tieleman et al., 2018). The next section takes a closer look at economics in secondary education and the subsequent one considers university education.

Economics in secondary education

The aim of this section is to offer further critical insight into how the subject of economics in education and in schools is taught and learned. The general picture is that economics in secondary education is still dictated by traditional economic theories. It is argued that this may undermine some very important perspectives that are needed for pupils to understand better the economic lives we all live as part of our present living conditions, for instance, the need to work.

Important objectives of teachers in secondary school economics include helping their pupils to gain a basic level of economic literacy and to prepare them for future academic economics education (e.g., Grol, 2016; Siegfried et al., 2010). As an example, the national voluntary content standards for pre-college economics in the United States aim at 'increasing the likelihood that the next generation of adults will understand the powerful fundamental principles of economics' (Siegfried and Meszaros, 1997: 253). The original version of these Standards was published in 1997. It sums up 20 fundamental economic concepts, varying from *scarcity* in Standard 1, to *markets* in Standard 8, and does not put much emphasis on factual knowledge about real-world economies (Siegfried and Meszaros, 1997). The second edition of these Standards, published by the US Council for Economic Education in 2010, introduces, amongst others, 'increasingly frequent observations by behavioural economists of some predictable patterns of producer and consumer behaviour that contradict the traditional paradigm of rational wealth maximising individuals' (Siegfried et al., 2010: vii). Despite this recent revision, the voluntary content standards still 'reflect the view of a large majority of economists today in favour of a "neoclassical model" of economic behaviour' (Siegfried et al., 2010: vi). The dominance of the neoclassical approach to economics is also present in other economics curricula for secondary education in, for example, the United Kingdom (Department for Education, 2014), parts of Germany (Stolze, 2011), and the Netherlands (Teulings et al., 2015). In line with the developments within economics described earlier in this chapter, Grol (2016) advocates the incorporation of insights from behavioural economics in secondary education, as this may increase the ability of pupils to improve their economic literacy.

But why may this be a helpful idea? As an example, do you remember the career services offered by your school? Typically, these are based on the assumption that you are an essentially rational being who makes calculated decisions and choices to secure a financially secure future, and education is there, partly, to serve this purpose. Moreover, a neoclassical approach within an economics class more or less reduces the complexity of human behaviour to a model in which *homo economicus* reaches optimal decisions (Bruni and Sugden, 2007; Cartwright, 2011). Models, by definition, are simplified representations of merely parts of real economic behaviour or phenomena (Boumans and Davis, 2010; Mäki, 2005; Morgan, 2005). As such, this neoclassical perspective may be helpful when preparing pupils for future college economics. However, a *homo economicus* has seldom been seen making real-world decisions. Hence, the extent to which its use may be helpful when aiming at gaining a basic level of economic literacy may be questioned.

Economics at the university level

Far into the nineteenth century, university professors in the United States offered students courses in political economy. This subject was grounded in moral philosophy and aimed at studying production, trade and national wealth. Political economy had 'to fit into the summation along with ethics, logic, moral principles, religious insight, the lessons of history' (Parrish, 1967: 2) and was considered a rather vague subject. The dominant teaching/learning method used during these courses can be characterised as *recitation*: students studied texts and recited these to a professor. At the end of the nineteenth century, many US students picked up economics classes in Germany, the academic centre of the world at that time, as they were interested in studying the causes underlying the extraordinary developments of the German economy (Parrish, 1967). These students also encountered teaching/learning methods in Germany that appeared refreshingly new to them. These included seminars during which the professor talked and students listened. Back in the United States, these experiences were transformed into teaching/learning activities that allowed for, amongst others, discussions on economics topics amongst students and their professors, and individual research projects by students who were guided by their professors during that process (Parrish, 1967). Within economics '[s]cientific investigation became the authority. [...] Professional skills in research, analysis, presentation, became more important than the accumulation of facts' (Parrish, 1967: 11). More research meant more literature, more professors, and more jobs for economists. This contributed to the professionalisation and maturation of economics as a scientific discipline at US universities. Until far into the twentieth century, economics was a broad science with many competing views. In the second half of the twentieth century. However, the neoclassical approach discussed earlier became the dominant paradigm in economics.

Today, economics education at the university level aims at fostering educational goals related to, for example, 'develop[ing] students' competence in the assimilation of complex arguments, the analysis of practical issues, logical thought, quantitative techniques, mathematical skills, and effective communication' (University of Cambridge, 2019: 1). Introductory courses in economics at Cambridge University, for example, include basic knowledge of, amongst others, rationality, markets, institutions, elementary models, and statistical analysis. Although the level of complexity is far more advanced than economics in secondary education, the similarity it bears is the fairly dominant neoclassical character of the content of college economics.

Three general patterns can be found in the education of economics at the university level: (1) the dominance of one way of thinking; (2) the focus on quantitative skills; and (3) the lack of attention to the real world. This is confirmed by various studies that have been conducted in the United Kingdom (Earle *et al.*, 2016; Cambridge Society for Economic Pluralism, 2014; Post-Crash Economics Society, 2014; Svenlén *et al.*, 2018), France (Government of France, 2014; PEPS-Economie Students' Association, 2014), Germany (Fauser and Kaskel, 2016), the Netherlands (Tieleman *et al.*, 2018), and the United States (Neilson, 2010). Let us elaborate these patterns.

First, economics education at universities is dominated by one way of thinking. This expresses itself in various ways. With regard to economic theory, almost all attention is devoted to neoclassical economics. In the Netherlands, for example, 86 per cent of the theory courses is devoted to neoclassical economics. No other approach is treated in a serious manner. Feminist economics, for example, receives only one per cent of the teaching time (Tieleman *et al.*, 2018). Education is mainly organised in a way to make students think along the lines of neoclassical economics. This approach to economics education is often promoted under the slogan 'thinking like an economist', with an implicit reference to a neoclassical economist. Critical thinking is discouraged, while conformity is encouraged. This is also reflected in the teaching materials and testing methods. The reliance on textbooks is very high. And exams mainly focus on the reproduction of knowledge, not on independent judgement and reflection on economic questions (Earle *et al.*, 2016). Furthermore, relatively little attention is paid to other disciplines, such as politics, sociology and history.

Second, quantitative skills receive a lot of attention. As noted earlier, economics is often presented as the hardest social science because of its strong reliance on quantitative research methods. Mathematics is also used as selection mechanism, either as formal requirement to enter the programme or in courses in which students that encounter difficulties with mathematics are encouraged to switch to another study. The cornerstone of economics education is learning to work with abstract theoretical mathematical models. Most of the testing thus focuses on whether students are able to manipulate a model (Earle *et al.*, 2016). The focus on quantitative skills, however, leads to a neglect of qualitative features. In the Netherlands, only 2 per cent of methods courses is devoted to qualitative research methods, while 98 per cent covers statistics and mathematics (Tieleman *et al.*, 2018). Because of this focus on numbers, economists encounter difficulties when dealing with qualitative aspects of the economy, such as institutions, culture, and emotions.

Third, there is a lack of attention to the real world. There is a preference for technique over content, and analytic rigour over relevance. This also reflected in the prominent position of quantitative skills discussed above. It often leads to precise analyses which ignore highly important factors, such as context, culture, and institutions. Economics education seems to have turned Read's (1898) argument upside down, as it seems to advocate that it is better to be *exactly wrong* than *vaguely right*. In the Netherlands, 75 per cent of all courses are purely theoretical and lack any attention to the real world, such as the big economic challenges of our time, economic history and knowledge about specific economic sectors (Tieleman *et al.*, 2018).

In 2011, students walked out of Professor Mankiw's economics class at Harvard University in the United States to express their discontent with, and concerns about how they were educated. According to their open letter in the *Harvard Political Review*, the introductory course in economics lacked a 'critical discussion of both the benefits and flaws of different economic simplifying models' (Harvard Political Review, 2011). Being aware of their major positions later on in life, the students add that: 'If Harvard fails to equip its students with a broad and critical understanding of economics, their actions are likely to harm the global financial system. The last five years of economic turmoil have been proof enough of this' (Harvard Political Review, 2011). Acknowledging the importance of broad and pluralistic economic education perhaps cannot be stated more clearly than by these privileged students themselves. Although it must be noted that a broad and pluralistic education of economics is important at *all* levels – and could therefore start with enriching the introductory courses in economics at the level of secondary education.

Conclusion

Economics as a discipline offers multiple perspectives, approaches, and views that have developed over time. The neoclassical approach dominates economics education in secondary schools and at universities around the globe. New insights, for example from behavioural, institutional, or evolutionary economists, try to re(de)fine parts of neoclassical theory. Moreover, within the research frontier one may observe conservatives who seek to strengthen the foundations of neoclassical economics, revisionists who seek to modify it, and revolutionaries who call for a complete overhaul. As this chapter has clarified, these developments have made their way into the education of economics in a very limited manner. Economics education in tilting too much towards neoclassical economics might not suffice to understand the complex social and economic realities in which we live today. Student movements feel the urge to contribute actively to the process of incorporating such insights more prominently in economics curricula worldwide.

> **Questions for reflection**
>
> 1. How would *homo economicus* decide whether or not to buy a hot dog when (s)he walks by a food truck? Please describe this process carefully by referring to, at least, the concepts of *perfect rationality* and *self-interest*.
> 2. By changing the concept of *perfect rationality* into the concept of *bounded rationality*, how would the decision-making process you have just described be influenced?
> 3. Please identify possible advantages and shortcomings of using *homo economicus* when trying to understand economic choices and decisions.
> 4. Following a *neoclassical line of reasoning*, why do you think Alan Greenspan expected 'that the self-interest of organizations, especially banks and others, was the best way to protect shareholders, capital, and business'?
> 5. Please elaborate the importance of leaving behind the *recitation* teaching/learning method at universities for the maturation of economics as a scientific discipline in the United States.
> 6. What is your view on the position that economics education could benefit from a more *pluralist* approach, as pointed out at several moments throughout this chapter?
> 7. When studying *education*, what do you think an economist could contribute? Which kind of approach could be beneficial? How?

Summary points

- Economics as a discipline offers multiple perspectives, approaches, and views that have developed over time.
- The neoclassical approach to economics is dominant in economics education in secondary schools and at universities around the globe.
- Upcoming insights, for example from behavioural economists, try to re(de)fine parts of neo-classical theory.
- Student movements feel the urge to contribute actively to the process of incorporating such insights more prominently in economics curricula worldwide.

Recommended readings

Chang, H. (2014) *Economics: The User's Guide*. London: Bloomsbury Press.
Fischer, L., Hasell, J., Proctor, J., Uwakwe, D., Ward-Perkins, Z. and Watson, C. (2017) *Rethinking Economics*. Abingdon: Routledge.
Kahneman, D. (2012) *Thinking, Fast and Slow*. London: Penguin Press.
Raworth, K. (2018) *Doughnut Economics: Seven Ways to Think Like a 21st-Century Economist*. New York: Random House Business.

References

Angner, E. (2012) *A Course in Behavioral Economics*. New York: Palgrave Macmillan.
Blair, M.M. (2011) An economic perspective on the notion of 'human capital'. In A. Burton-Jones and J.-C. Spender (eds.), *The Oxford Handbook of Human Capital*. Oxford: Oxford University Press.
Boumans, M. and Davis, J. (2010) *Economic Methodology*. New York: Palgrave Macmillan.
Bruni, L. and Sugden, R. (2007) The road not taken: how psychology was removed from economics, and how it might be brought back. *Economic Journal*, 117, pp. 146–173.
Cambridge Society for Economic Pluralism (2014) *CSEP Survey of Economics Students: Is it Time for Change at Cambridge?* Available at: http://www.cambridgepluralism.org/uploads/1/7/4/9/17499733/report_v14_w.appendix.pdf (Accessed 17 July 2019).
Camerer, C. (1999) Behavioral economics: reunifying psychology and economics. *Proceedings of the National Academy of Science*, 96, pp. 10575–10577.
Camerer, C. (2005) *Behavioral Economics*. In: World Congress of the Econometric Society, 18–24 August, London.
Camerer, C., Loewenstein, G. and Rabin, M. (2004) *Advances in Behavioral Economics*. Princeton: Princeton University Press.
Cartwright, E. (2011) *Behavioral Economics*. Abingdon: Routledge.
Colander, D. (2005) The making of an economist redux. *Journal of Economic Perspectives*, 19(1), pp. 175–198.
Colander, D., Holt, R. and Rosser, J. (2010) *The Changing Face of Economics: Conversations with Cutting Edge Economists*. Ann Arbor: University of Michigan Press.
De Graaf, F. (2010) Economics, scientific doubt and history. *EFMD Global*, 4, pp. 48–51.
De Muijnck, S. and Sent, E.-M. (2018) *In What Direction Is Economics Heading?* (Working paper). Nijmegen: Radboud University.
Department for Education (2014) *GCE AS and A Level Subject Content for Economics*. London: DfE.
Earle, J., Moral, C. and Ward-Perkins, Z. (2016) *The Econocracy: The Perils of Leaving Economics to the Experts*. Oxford: Oxford University Press.
Engelhardt, L. (2011) *Behavioral Economics: An Overview for Principles of Microeconomics Students* (Working paper). Available at: www.lucasmengelhardt.com/yahoo_site_admin/assets/docs/BehavioralEconomics.24194115.pdf (Accessed 17 July 2019).
Fauser, H. and Kaskel, M. (2016) *Pluralism in Economics Teaching in Germany: Evidence from a New Dataset*. Available at: www.boeckler.de/pdf/v_2016_10_21_fauser.pdf (Accessed 17 July 2019).
Fourcade, M., Ollion, E. and Algan, Y. (2015) The superiority of economists. *Journal of Economic Perspectives*, 29(1), pp. 89–114.
Frank, R., Gilovich, T. and Regan, D. (1993) Does studying economics inhibit cooperation? *Journal of Economic Perspectives*, 7(2), pp. 159–171.
Friedman, M. (1966) *Essays in Positive Economics*. Chicago: University of Chicago Press.
Government of France (2014) *L'avenir des Sciences Economiques a l'Universite en France*. Available at: https://cache.media.enseignementsup-recherche.gouv.fr/file/Formations_et_diplomes/05/1/Rapport_Hautcoeur2014_328051.pdf (Accessed 17 July 2019).
Grol, R. (2016) Investigating Economic Classroom Experiments. Doctoral dissertation, Radboud University, Nijmegen.
Grol, R., Sent, E.M. and de Vries, B. (2017) Participate or observe? Effects of economic classroom experiments on students' economic literacy. *European Journal of Psychology of Education*, 32(2), pp. 289–310.
Harvard Political Review (2011) *An Open Letter to Greg Mankiw* (2 November 2011). Available at: http://harvardpolitics.com/harvard/an-open-letter-to-greg-mankiw/ (Accessed 17 July 2019).
Heukelom, F. (2011) Behavioral economics. In J. Davies and D. Hands (eds.), *The Elgar Companion to Recent Economic Methodology*. Cheltenham: Edward Elgar.
Heukelom, F. (2014) *Behavioral Economics: A History*. Cambridge: Cambridge University Press.
Kahneman, D. (2003) A psychological perspective on economics. *American Economic Review*, 93(2), pp. 162–168.
Mäki, U. (2005) Models are experiments, experiments are models. *Journal of Economic Methodology*, 12(2), pp. 303–315.
Mankiw, N. and Scarth, W. (2012) *Macroeconomics*. New York: W.H. Freeman.
Marwell, G. and Ames, R. (1981) Economists free ride, does anyone else? Experiments on the provision of public goods. *Journal of Public Economics*, 15(3), pp. 295–310.

Morgan, M. (2005) Experiments versus models: New phenomena, interference and surprise. *Journal of Economic Methodology*, 12(2), pp. 317–329.

Morgan, M. and Rutherford, M. (eds.) (1998) *From Interwar Pluralism to Postwar Neoclassicism*. Durham, NC: Duke University Press.

Neilson, D. (2010) *U.S. Undergraduate Economics Education*. Available at: www.ineteconomics.org/uploads/downloads/Existing_econ_curriculum_US.pdf (Accessed 17 July 2019).

Parrish, J. (1967) Rise of economics as an academic discipline: the formative years to 1900. *Southern Economic Journal*, 34(1), pp. 1–16.

PEPS-Economie Students' Association (2014) The case for pluralism: what French undergraduate economics teaching is all about and how it can be improved. *International Journal of Pluralism and Economics Education*, 5(4), pp. 385–400.

Post-Crash Economics Society (2014) *Economics, Education and Unlearning: Economics Education at the University of Manchester*. Manchester: University of Manchester.

Read, C. (1898) *Logic, Deductive and Inductive*. London: A. Moring.

Robbins, L. (1935) *An Essay on the Nature and Significance of Economic Science*. London: Macmillan.

Santos, A. (2011) Experimental economics. In J. Davies and D. Hands (eds.), *The Elgar Companion to Recent Economic Methodology*. Cheltenham: Edward Elgar.

Schotter, A. (2003) *Microeconomics: A Modern Approach* (3rd edition). Upper Saddle River: Prentice Hall.

Sent, E.-M. (2004) Behavioral economics: how psychology made its (limited) way back into economics. *History of Political Economy*, 36(4), pp. 735–760.

Siegfried, J. and Meszaros, B. (1997) National voluntary content standards for pre-college economics education. *American Economic Review*, 87(2), pp. 247–253.

Siegfried, J., Krueger, A., Collins, S., Frank, R., MacDonald, R., McGoldrick, K., Taylor, J. and Vredeveld, G. (2010) *Voluntary Content Standards in Economics* (2nd edition). Available at: www.councilforeconed.org/wp/wp-content/uploads/2012/03/voluntary-national-content-standards-2010.pdf (Accessed 27 March 2013).

Simon, H. (1959) Theories of decision-making in economics and behavioral science. *American Economic Review*, 49(3), pp. 253–283.

Stolze, R. (ed.) (2011) *Bildungsplan Wirtschaft Freie und Hansestadt Hamburg [Economics curriculum for the Free and Hanseatic City of Hamburg]*. Hamburg: Behörde für Schule und Berufsbildung.

Svenlén, S., Sargent, E., Tyler, G. and Pedersen, O. (2018) *Educating Economists? A Report on the Economics Education at Durham University*. Durham, NC: Durham Society for Economic Pluralism.

Telegraph (2008) The Queen asks why no one saw the credit crunch coming [5 November 2008]. Available at: www.telegraph.co.uk/news/uknews/theroyalfamily/3386353/The-Queen-asks-why-no-one-saw-the-credit-crunch-coming.html (Accessed 17 July 2019).

Teulings, C. et al. (2005) *The Wealth of Education*. Available at: www.econnet.nl/vecon/onderwijs/teulings/eindrapport.pdf (Accessed 17 July 2019).

Tieleman, J., De Muijnck, S., Kavelaars, M. and Oostmeijer, F. (2012) *Thinking Like an Economist? A Quantitative Analysis of Economics Bachelor Curricula in the Netherlands*. Available at: www.rethinkingeconomics.nl/uploads/5/3/2/2/53228883/thinking_like_an_economist__2_.docx (Accessed 17 July 2019).

Tugwell, R. (1922) Human nature in economic theory. *Journal of Political Economy*, 30(3), pp. 317–345.

Tversky, A. and Kahneman, D. (1974) Judgment under uncertainty: Heuristics and biases. *Science*, 185, pp. 1124–1131.

University of Cambridge (2019) *Why Choose Economics*. Available at: www.econ.cam.ac.uk/apply/ba-economics/why-choose-economics (Accessed 17 July 2019).

Van Staveren, I. (2014) *Economics after the Crisis: An Introduction to Economics from a Pluralist and Global Perspective*. Abingdon: Routledge.

Weber, R. and Camerer, C. (2006) 'Behavioral experiments' in economics. *Experimental Economics*, 9, pp. 187–192.

Wigstrom, C. (2016) *A Survey of Undergraduate Economics Programmes in the UK*. Available at: www.ineteconomics.org/uploads/downloads/existing_undergrad_econ_curriculum_UK.pdf (Accessed 17 July 2019).

Wilkinson, N. and Klaes, M. (2011) *An Introduction to Behavioral Economics* (2nd edition). Basingstoke: Palgrave Macmillan.

3 Elementary education and child labour
From economic to ecological histories of modern childhood

David Blundell

Introduction

Ninth August 2020 marks 150 years since the passage of the landmark 1870 Elementary Education Act for England and Wales. This significant anniversary comes at a time when the world faces multiple grave concerns, amongst which the impacts of human-induced climate change and the associated threat of mass species extinction must be paramount. Human life and society flourished under relatively stable environmental conditions identified as the Holocene that followed the retreat of ice-caps some 11,500 years ago; however, many scientists now consider that human agency has wrought such profound impacts on the Earth and its systems that we now inhabit the Anthropocene wherein environmental stability is increasingly uncertain. This invites an observation and a challenge: the observation being that in the Anthropocene the human and non-human (sometimes called 'natural') world are completely entangled and indistinguishable; and, so it follows that we are challenged to work out how societies and institutions can respond to the hitherto unencountered threats, problems, but (also perhaps) opportunities for learning that we face in this entangled reality. Education is charged with a unique role in meeting the scientific, political, social, cultural, and intellectual demands that these challenges present; however, this must go beyond merely tinkering with curriculum content and requires reconsideration of fundamental questions about human nature and the relations of humans to the natural world upon which institutional realities and relationships are founded. The ways in which we think about children, childhood and young people are fundamental to this task.

The Elementary Education Act 1870

On 17 February 1870 William Edward Forster, Liberal MP for Bradford and Vice-President of the Education Department in William Gladstone's government introduced a bill in the House of Commons to establish a framework for elementary schooling that would make attendance possible for all children in England and Wales. The bill received royal assent and passed into law on 9 August later that year. In Scotland a duty had been placed on local landowners to provide elementary education by the Scottish Parliament since 1633, a position that was reinforced administratively by the Education (Scotland) Act of 1872 that authorised the formation of School Boards in line with the developments in England and Wales. The 1870 Elementary Education (or 'Forster') Act steered a delicate course between parties pursuing educational reform, but motivated by differing interests, notably the radical National Education League with origins in the industrial heartland of Birmingham and the National Education Union of Manchester (Briggs, 1991: 231–245). Thus the 1870 Act relied upon an uneasy coalition between secular groups championing state education on the one hand and religious interests on the other, of which the Church of England was the largest alongside a range of non-conformist denominations and the smaller Catholic Poor School Committee (Pratt-Adams et al., 2010: 53). These religious interests were not based on untried principle; rather, the Church of England, Catholics, and non-conformists had provided 'voluntary' schooling for working-class children aided by government grant since the 1820s (Blundell, 2012, forthcoming). However, Forster estimated that this accounted for around just two-fifths of the children aged between six and ten, and a third between ten and twelve years. Forster's response is pragmatic: new provision and a comprehensive system of administration would be enabled through local School Boards, whilst existing provision would continue to be supported financially by the state, albeit subject to caveats that permitted parents to withdraw children from religious instruction on grounds of conscience and required that instruction be broadly Christian, but non-denominational. This pragmatism extended to Forster's formula for achieving comprehensive and geographically accessible schooling excessive expense:

> Our object is to complete the present voluntary system, to fill up gaps, sparing the public money where it can. ... We take care that the country shall be properly mapped and divided, so that its wants may be duly ascertained. For this, we take present known divisions, and declare them to be school districts, so that upon the passing of this Bill there will be no portion of England or Wales not included in one school district or another.
>
> (Hansard, 1870: para. 444 to para. 445)

Forster sought not only to reassure taxpayers that money would be prudently disbursed, but also those he termed 'benevolent men' – such as Ashley Cooper, Lord Shaftesbury of the Ragged School Union – who championed the religious interest in redeeming lost souls. He also sought to secure the assistance of parents to obviate concerns that increased time spent in education reduced opportunities for paid labour and curtailed children's direct contribution to family income and economy. Although children continued to work after the passage of the 1870 Act, Forster's Elementary Education Act wrought a transformation in popular consensus surrounding where children should be found between the end of infancy and the onset of adolescence. Thus, schooling became the dominant institution regulating children's lives beyond the home. The effect was to construct a near-universal childhood experience with the child as phenotype for a distinctive category of personhood. As Pamela Horn notes, the particular visibility afforded children as the effects of Forster's Act gathered momentum meant that it served as the first of:

> no less than twenty Acts in the educational sphere alone between 1870 and 1900, as well as a wide range of other legislation ... [that] had begun a process whereby the position of the child had changed from that of being one of the least considered members of society to one receiving a safer passage through the vulnerable years of immaturity and some opportunity to prepare for the responsibilities of adult life.
>
> (Horn, 1994: 68)

Whilst the increasing domination of children's time and the growing consensus around school as their proper location curtailed their direct financial contribution to family income, it should not be inferred that Forster's Act obviated children's contribution to the economic sphere, nor concerns about their contribution to the reproduction of wealth or imperial interests. Rather, the emerging child-adult binary encouraged by universal schooling reinforced a view of childhood as a period of deferred economic interest. Signally, Forster stresses the competitive advantage mass education could afford the nation and thus the economic contribution that schooled children would make in time as educated, and thus 'useful', adults:

> We must not delay. Upon the speedy provision of elementary education depends our industrial prosperity ... uneducated labourers – and many of our labourers are utterly uneducated – are, for the most part, unskilled labourers, and ... they will become over-matched in the competition of the world.
>
> (Hansard, 1870: para. 466)

Forster's arguments for the extension of education via his bill were not solely economic ones, but stress the contribution education must make to meeting the political and constitutional challenges presented by the turn towards what he calls 'popular government' accompanying the recent extension of electoral rights to some working-class males in the Great Reform Act of 1867 under the Liberal Prime Minister, William Ewart Gladstone. This limited extension of the franchise to male heads of household (all women and other working-class males remained unable to vote) undoubtedly contributed to Gladstone's victory in the General Election of 1868. When Forster states that '[t]here are questions demanding answers, problems which must be solved, which ignorant constituencies are ill-fitted to solve', he is expressing concern about extending the electoral franchise before voters are sufficiently educated. For the historian of the nineteenth century, Asa Briggs, these concerns mark a mid-century shift in focus for middle-class anxieties surrounding education:

> [d]uring the last two decades of the nineteenth century attitudes towards education and society changed as much as attitudes towards other aspects of organisation and policy, with H. G. Wells ... playing a prominent part in shifting the terms of the debate about education and class to middle-class/working-class relationships. The Education Act of 1870 was for him 'an act to educate the lower classes for employment on lower class lines, and with specially trained inferior teachers'.
>
> (Briggs, 1991: 241–242)

Demonstrating perhaps that if, as Horn suggests, there was a new sensibility surrounding childhood and children's relation to economic activity, it was distinctly caveated with respect to working-class children. Forster's injunction to act speedily to rectify the democratic and educational shortcomings of working-class voters is lent extra force by perceived external threats to Britain's imperial pre-eminence posed by other '[c]ivilized communities throughout the world [which] are massing themselves together' – a thinly-veiled but distinctly ominous reference to German unification under Otto von Bismarck – and the assertion that: '... if we are to hold our position among men of our own race or among the nations of the world we must make up for the smallness of our numbers by increasing the intellectual force of the individual' (Hansard, 1870: para. 466). It should be said that the Prussians and French had introduced systems of mass education at the beginning of the nineteenth century, and so this could be seen as a belated exercise in catching up. Furthermore, the British Empire was at this time without equal as a geographically extensive, wealthy and powerful imperial entity, so to suggest vulnerability on grounds of 'smallness of numbers' seems odd at best, but more likely, typically dismissive of Britain's overseas' subjects and their exclusion from the notion of 'nation'. Forster's concatenation of the economic, political and social prosperity of the nation with that of education and schooling continued to find an echo in subsequent legislation, and reiterates Horn's point about the ensuing rash of educational legislation before 1900. Public health measures introduced in the wake of the humiliations inflicted on the British army during the South African Wars (1899–1902) recognised this linkage, and the School Medical Service formed in 1907 was able to exploit the access to the nation's children that mass schooling afforded (Blundell, 2012). H.A.L. Fisher, when introducing the bill (in 1917) that would become the 1918 Education Act, makes reference to the ongoing conflict with Germany – a stark echo of the anxieties voiced by Forster in 1870 – when arguing for greater attention to the welfare of young children and for a programme of universal secondary education in response not only to the requirements of industry, but also to a demand enhanced popular citizenship that wartime social solidarity had encouraged. That said, meeting the requirements of industry may not sit comfortably with educational curricula centred on citizenship, social solidarity and the fulfilment of human potential that may invite criticality and challenges to normative assumptions. Indeed, this disjunction between economic and political goals represents a continuing fault line running through popular education and arguments surrounding its purpose.

Child labour, elementary schooling and the invention of modern childhood

Forster charged education with a high commission as contributor to the widest possible economic, political and social interests of the nation. In the process, as Harry Hendrick demonstrates, the 1870 Elementary Education Act made its contribution to a sea change in popular attitudes towards children and childhood over the course of the nineteenth century:

> In 1800 the meaning of childhood was ambiguous and not universally in demand. By 1914 the uncertainty had been virtually resolved and the identity largely determined, to the satisfaction of the middle and the respectable working class. A recognizably 'modern' notion of childhood was in place: it was legally, legislatively, socially, medically, psychologically, educationally and politically institutionalized.
>
> (Hendrick, 1997: 30)

Estimates suggest that between a quarter and a half of children received some measure of schooling prior to Forster's 1870 Act; however, as Hendrick suggests, the legislation went beyond merely increasing the proportion of children in schooling, and was central in reconstructing childhood as an ideologically modern entity marked by the material, institutional, and social phenomenology with which we are broadly familiar. This reconstruction effected a transformation in the meaning of childhood as a time of moral as well as spatial separation from forms of labour associated with monetarily-remunerated work. With reference to the United States, but having wider relevance, the sociologist and economic historian Viviana Zelizer described what she saw as a growing 'sacralisation' of children during the latter years of the nineteenth and early twentieth centuries (Zelizer, 1994). Through this, children and childhood took on an idealised, quasi-sacred status in the popular imagination; so that widespread acceptance of children's economic value in the form of family income was increasingly displaced by a conviction that the child was 'emotionally priceless' and thus childhood should be properly demarcated as antithetical to monetary labour. The American poet Charles M. Dickinson touched an enthusiastic popular nerve when in 1904 he wrote:

> They are idols of heart and of household;
> They are angels of God in disguise;
> His sunlight still sleeps in their tresses,
> His glory still gleams in their eyes.
>
> (Dickinson, 'The Children', 1889)

As much as the separation of children from the adult world by schooling and other institutions encouraged this ideological turn towards a recognisably modern and universalised childhood, it also marked that separation via a distinction between the child-saving virtues of school *work* and the moral vices of child *labour*. Hendrick (1997) illustrates the impact of this moral turn with reference to Victorian concerns surrounding 'the delinquent child' as embodiment for moral jeopardy. The delinquent child knew and had seen too much of the world and its viciousness, an argument where 'too much' was calibrated by direct contrast with the sacralised *childlike* child.

The shifting meanings and eventual transformation in both attitudes to and provision for childhood identified by Hendrick on the eve of the First World War contrast with popular views on children and work in the eighteenth and well into the nineteenth century. Notably, because not only was work an everyday reality for children of the labouring poor, but also there was little evidence that this featured as a cause for concern. Indeed, labouring families' concerns, particularly in agricultural and rural areas, were more likely to revolve around finding sufficient work for their offspring as demographic and economic circumstances changed. This meant that household budgets often failed to cover the modest fees required by the correspondingly modest calibre of schooling available to them. Changing economic conditions in the eighteenth century accompanied demographic shifts that saw a marked increase in the proportion of the population under 15, from 28.5 per cent in 1671 to a high point of 39.6 per cent in 1826 and thereafter to hover in the high 30s until the century's close. Thus Great Britain's population was growing and increasingly youthful (Horn, 1994: 4–5). However, in many rural areas the growth in the juvenile population coincided with labour-saving reforms affecting agricultural production, meaning that there were fewer jobs available and children's unemployment and under-employment became commonplace.

In mercantile cities, such as London, children might work in relatively small-scale workshop settings, perhaps alongside family members, or they found casual employment in one-off or 'piece-work' activities, such as box-making, clothing manufacture, running errands, or minding market stalls. These activities were largely the preserve of boys; by contrast, the position for female children was employment in less visible domestic tasks at home or in service. There were, however, other growing industries and trades where large numbers of boys and girls were required and found employment. The volume of activity led to these activities becoming causes for popular concern as the industrial revolution swept the land and the new childhood sensibility, referred to above, took hold. These activities included the employment of young children in coal mining and in the mechanised factories of the nation's burgeoning textile industries; however, it was the plight of the juvenile chimney sweep (otherwise known as the 'climbing boys') that attained the status of a *cause celebre*. In mining, the age at which young children might be employed varied with local circumstances; in North Staffordshire a partial deferral was typical and few children younger than 13 went underground (albeit because of competition with the pottery industry, that took children from 8 years old), whereas in the south part of that county it was common for children aged 7 to go underground (ibid.: 8). With around 20 per cent of the cotton spinning workforce in 1816 comprising children under the age of 13, textile mills generated concern over the sheer number employed in relation to adult workers. Small children were employed to work in confined spaces where they made adjustments and running repairs to moving machinery and rapidly-rotating drive apparatus. In the process these children were prey to horrific injuries in addition to the wear-and-tear on growing bodies that accompanied hard manual labour (ibid.: 6).

Concerns over the conditions in which child chimney-sweeps lived and worked were raised in the early 1760s. In spite of the terrifying darkness, risks of falling, or the carcinogenic properties of soot, not to mention abrasions on elbows and knees, small boys were routinely employed as cheap labour to sweep the chimneys of a growing urban populace. These boys might typically be drawn from the ranks of parish paupers and apprenticed to a sweep without much regard to their working conditions. Several attempts from 1788 were made to regulate the practice before 'climbing' was at length abolished as late as 1875. Pamela Horn notes that, although the actual number of boys was small in comparison with those in other industrial settings (perhaps 550 in London and according to the contemporary campaigner Lord Ashley Cooper, Earl of Shaftesbury around 4,000 nationwide), attempts to curtail or ban this form of child labour were consistently evaded by employers (ibid.: 17).

As part of their campaigning, those who sought to abolish these forms of labour encouraged comparisons with the position of child slaves in Britain's overseas colonies; indeed, these comparisons surface in complaints by the children themselves. One such complainant was Joseph Hebergam, who began work in a worsted spinning mill near Huddersfield at the age of seven and for whom a daily routine lasting from 5am to 8pm was urged on by violent strappings by his overseer. Recounting, as an adult in the 1830s, his move aged 10 from the worsted mill to another more brutal factory with longer hours, Joseph cited how 'I wished many times they would have sent me for a West India slave … I thought … that there could not be worse slaves than those who worked in factories' (Cunningham, 2006: 158). Work by the historian Audra Diptee has revealed the scale of young children's inclusion in transportation and sale into slavery within the Atlantic slave trade and the brutal processes by which an enslaved populace was sustained and reproduced for the benefit of owners (Diptee, 2007). Notwithstanding Hebergam's sentiments and the cruelties he experienced, Diptee observes that such comparisons overlooked or downplayed a vital difference, in that the

> vast majority of labourers in Jamaica were enslaved and those in Britain were not. The slave status of Jamaican child labourers meant that they were not subjects of the British crown but, in fact, were legally defined as the property of subjects to the crown.
>
> (Diptee, 2007: 53)

Arguably, such comparisons were drawn for rhetorical effect rather than being justified by the brutal facts; however, they perhaps reveal a nation grappling simultaneously with questions around the dehumanisation of enslaved people on grounds of race, as well as of age and immaturity. It should be noted, however, that restrictions on children's work were not welcomed by all; signally, Karl Marx challenged the legitimacy of characterising children's work through its worst manifestations and argued for the benefits flowing from combining education with work (Horn, 1994: 65). Furthermore, many parents and children objected, believing that, as one complainant put it, compulsory schooling turned 'useful people' to 'useless' as their financial contribution to the family income was curtailed or denied (Zelizer, 1994).

A milestone in the process of abolition of child labour is reached when the Royal Commission, to which Joseph Hebergam was giving evidence, led to the passage of the 1833 Factory Act. As with the climbing boys, attempts to pass legislation regulating children's employment in factories had been made before this, but, again, the effectiveness of the 1833 Act derived from the commitment to making it enforceable through a system of inspection. The act made it illegal to employ a child under age nine in a factory, and under 14 the eight hours they worked had to be matched by time in school – leading to the 'half-time' system that prevailed in many places well into the early twentieth century – so that by 1880 when the 'Mundella' Elementary Education Act made schooling compulsory up to age 10, the construction of a *proper childhood* as a separate condition from, and even oppositional to, manual labour had gained widespread acceptance as an appropriate aspiration (Cunningham, 2006). Over the subsequent century the minimum school leaving age was extended: to 11 in 1893; 12 in 1899; 14 years in 1918 with opportunities for working-class children to gain a scholarship and access to grammar school; 15 in 1947; and 16 in 1970. Subsequent measures have effectively raised the school leaving age or maintained a status of 'pupilhood' for many young people to 18 years by an insistence that all must be in some form of education, employment or training; furthermore, changes in rates of participation in HE mean that many young people now remain in full-time education beyond age 21. As the leaving age has increased, so the age at which state interest in children's education and care begins has extended over the past 20 years through programmes such as *Sure Start* and *Every Child Matters* and, more recently, the provision of free childcare for two-year-olds. This expansion of the educational sphere has also reinforced the construction of modern childhood as a distinctive spatial, temporal, and material phenomenon calibrated by the ladder-like age-grading that is structurally integral to the forms of schooling inherited from the Victorians. However, childhood as a standardised condition can sit awkwardly with children's lived experience and their position within diverse social worlds. Consequently, despite the dominant role played by schooling in shaping the meaning of childhood and regulating children's time and spatial range, it would be naive to suggest that these measures entirely insulate young people, especially those in the years of adolescence onward, from work or working life. This is true for many children in economically wealthy societies of the minority world – such as Britain – but commonplace for children and young people within the majority world where conflicts between the opportunities afforded by education and the brute economic necessity to undertake paid labour can be acute.

Education, development goals and contemporary children's work

In 2015 the United Nations General Assembly ratified 17 global Sustainable Development Goals (SDGs) to guide development across a broad front between then and the year 2030. The fourth of these goals is the provision of 'Quality Education' which commits signatories to 'Ensure inclusive and equitable quality education and promote lifelong learning opportunities for all'. The SDGs built on the eight Millennium Development Goals (MDGs) ratified by the UN in 2000, whose second goal was to 'achieve universal primary education'.

Running through these initiatives is a presumption, barely challenged since the mid-Victorian era, that schooling offers children opportunities to transcend their existing circumstances and removes them from the harsh vicissitudes of labour. Moreover, the inclusion of these goals under the heading 'development' immediately locates education as a key contributor to the economic and social sphere alongside other quality of life, well-being, environmental and resource-management components. For Karen Wells, these widely accepted assumptions are lent justification by HCT and its claim:

> that people should be considered as a form of capital analogous in its importance for economic growth to any other kind of capital formation. To accumulate human capital is to increase the quality of human attributes through investing in nutrition, health, and knowledge and skill acquisition. Although human capital theory includes investments in health and nutrition, it is education that has been analysed as the key investment.
>
> (Wells, 2009: 98)

In practice, HCT relies on an implicit dualism between education and work, which privileges the former and all too frequently reduces the latter to 'child labour', with its pejorative connotations. Thus, in Wells' view, although campaigns against child labour frequently characterise abolition as a human rights intervention, the broader interests of economic development are in play, so that improving '… school attendance is seen as closely linked to how to stop children working and, logically, children working are seen as an obstacle to the formation of human capital' (ibid.: 98). In an inversion of the complaint by nineteenth-century children and families that compulsory elementary education turned them from 'useful' to 'useless', HCT promotes a near-universal conviction (expressed by the MDGs and SDGs) surrounding the *usefulness* of schooling and the *uselessness* of work or labour (see Chapter 7).

HCT identifies *the pupil* as the ideal role allotted to children; however, as Anne Trine Kjørholt vividly illustrates through the experience of Mary, aligning the aspiration to universal schooling with challenges encountered in the circumstances inhabited by children is far from straightforward. Kjørholt (2007) reported the experience of a young teenage woman growing up in the Philippines named Mary who had since childhood been caught between the necessity to earn money to support her family and a passionate desire to be at school whenever possible. Mary's dilemma was painfully revealed when she addressed a prestigious international conference marking the tenth anniversary of the ratification of the United Nations Convention on the Rights of the Child (UNCRC, 1989) in 1999. During an emotional address she pointed out that abolishing child labour would present her, and many like her, with an impossible conflict: Mary and her family need her income for basic necessities, but without it there was no prospect of paying for education. Consequently, her only option was to combine work with study through the night and whenever she could snatch opportunities.

Mary is not alone, and her experience not only points to a simple dualistic dilemma surrounding the abolition of child labour but also the complexity of children's lives as they struggle with circumstances over which they have limited control. For Karen Wells, this points to crucial questions of definition found in policy initiatives that serve as criteria by which not only to identify what is and is not considered acceptable, but also which forms of labour are rendered visible and thus the focus for action. Wells writes:

> According to the ILO [International Labour Organization] about one in five of the world's 1.5 billion children are involved in production either for the market of for their – or their families' – own use (ILO, 2006). Household chores, whether in the child's own or in someone else's home, do not count as economic activity.
>
> (Wells, 2009: 99)

The exclusion of household chores is controversial both because it underplays the physical demands and long hours that these can make on children, and because in many cases this work is the highly gendered preserve of female children. This underlines a pervasive feature of capitalism that regards the domestic sphere and the reproduction of labour as an economic 'externality', thereby compounding the subordination of women and girls within economic and social relations. Additionally, the ILO distinguishes between 'child work' – comprising a few hours light work per week between the ages 12 and 15 – and 'labour' that 'includes any work that has adverse effects on safety, physical or mental health and moral development, or excessive hours of work in any occupation, including one that is otherwise safe' (ibid.: 100). Harsh, dehumanising or criminally exploitative child labour cannot be defended; however, echoing Marx, Wells questions whether this is an appropriate benchmark against which children's work should be understood and evaluated. In actuality, the interpretation of what is and is not harmful, and to what degree, is often far from straightforward; so that, as Wells suggests, the assumption that schooling (beneficial thing) and work (harmful thing) represent simple polar opposites becomes questionable. Furthermore, is work always worse than being taught under inadequately resourced conditions by poorly qualified teachers, or even being subject to intolerable pressure to achieve and perform to meet externally imposed targets and league-table positions. For Wells, in the absence of a substantial body of research-based knowledge to which children themselves contribute, there is a tendency for debates about children and work to rely on sweeping generalisations that do not address knottier lived realities. Furthermore, at a philosophical and political level, should assumptions closely aligned to Western liberal notions of the individual self be uncritically applied in settings where family responsibility is paramount and more collective identities are the norm? As Mary's case illustrates, immediate necessities shape her life, and reductive moral binaries contribute little to resolving the challenges she faces. Finally, the reliance on HCT can mean that debates hinge on unspoken and partial assumptions about the purpose of human life: should work and schooling exhaust the dimensions by which children's lives are valorised? Might there also be a place for leisure and play with no purpose other than to enjoy association with friends and family?

Where now? From economic to ecological histories of modern childhood

In this chapter we have examined the pivotal role that schooling as an institution has played in the construction of 'modern childhood' as just one particular way to address social and economic priorities surrounding human biological immaturity. Key effects accompanying this institutionalisation have been: children's temporal and spatial separation from the wider social-world for significant periods of time; a rational ordering of childhood as an age-graded condition whose ladder-like telos is rationalised by staged developmental theories; and the deferral of children's economic engagement with the 'real-world' of adult concern. As we have seen with the case of Mary in the Philippines, the imperatives of work and labour sit awkwardly both with the institutionalised order of schooling and with the phenomenon of modern childhood.

This suggests a close linkage between economic conditions and the form childhood takes, with Mary's experience confirming that disparities can be stark in their effects. Acknowledging the uneasy interplay between such differences and commonalities became a major focus of the United Nation's Convention on the Rights of the Child (UNCRC, 1989). The Convention and debates around difference catalysed a multidisciplinary interest in childhood as a sociological, historical and spatial phenomenon that also challenged the sufficiency of developmental psychology in exhausting an understanding of children's lives. This emerging field of scholarly and professional endeavour was lent impetus by the publication of what Allison James and Alan Prout called 'a new paradigm for the sociology of childhood' (James and Prout, 1990: 7–34, and subsequent editions) that catalysed a wealth of interdisciplinary research and theoretical development.

The new paradigm advocated a social constructionist position that recognised differences in the meaning and practice of childhood in relation to ethnicity, class, and gender. Furthermore, it stressed the legitimacy of children's own standpoint on their worlds along with their active agency in ordering them. Taken as a whole, this work embraced a diverse interdisciplinary field to transcend sociology alone and is now usually identified as 'The New Social Studies of Childhood' (NSSC). Under the particular influence of feminist and post-colonial critical theory the NSSC has taken aim at pervasive assumptions surrounding the naturalness, universality, and historically-specific forms of rationality underpinning modern childhood to reveal not only the highly gendered terms found in a developmentalist understanding of growth but also their historical rootedness in the cultural and intellectual circumstances of modernity and the European Enlightenment. In a reflective paper entitled 'Why Children? Why Now?' Aitken *et al.* (2007) illustrate the discursive commonalities between child development as a system through which human capital is produced on the one hand, and development as a theoretical driver of Western-style economic progress and global market convergence on the other. Their paper suggests that, despite appearing to be concerned with disparate phenomena, they exhibit structural commonalities through a teleological approach that not only prescribes common destinations for material well-being and human progress, but also the path taken to reach them. These comparisons reveal 'development' to be a highly loaded and politically sensitive term through which a one-size-fits-all childhood is rationalised, and diversity in the form, content and values surrounding many children's lives is ignored or dismissed.

The theme of difference and childhood is taken up by Affrica Taylor (2013), an Australian geographer and early childhood specialist. Taylor demonstrates how closely embedded Australian aboriginal children are with their surrounding environment comprising animals and non-human others, that she calls *queer kin*. Because these children's experiences are very different, Taylor challenges the universality of Western-style, individualised childhoods along with assumptions about the meaning of nature that authorise them.

By questioning the continuing legitimacy of constructions of nature inherited from Enlightenment modernity, Taylor's work has commonalities with strands of *ecological* thought that indict the dualistic relationship between the human and the natural world. For ecological thinkers, recognising this dualism is fundamental to understanding the anthropogenic – or human-generated – environmental hazards we currently face because it authorised a conviction that humans are entitled to steward, control and improve the natural world to meet its material needs. Not only did this separate the human from non-human worlds but also authorised hierarchical distinctions between humans that legitimised racist, ethnocentric and sexist ideologies. Broadly speaking, these privileged the whiteness of European males and assigned to others varying degrees of subjection to nature and, by implication, a status as less civilised and lacking fully conscious rationality. Children were not immune from this hierarchical classification and here a youthful John Earle, future Bishop of Salisbury, expresses a commonplace view on children as closer to nature before their corruption by the world and its vices:

> A child is a man in a small Letter, Yet the best Copie of Adam before hee tasted of Eve, or the Apple. … Hee if natures fresh picture newly drawn in Oyle, which time and much handling, dimmes and defaces. His Soule is yet a white paper unscribled with observations of the world, wherewith at length it becomes a blurr'd Note-booke.
> (John Earle, *Microcosmographie*, 1628)

The corollary to these emerging assumptions of naturalness and innocence was that the child was characterised by weakness, incompleteness and limited rationality that required constant adult supervision and regulation, allowing ethnocentric and racist comparisons between children and non-Europeans, who were also deemed in need of stewardship, firm control and improvement.

However, our enveloping ecological crisis has encouraged a reconsideration of these assumptions about nature, with important implications for the currency of modern childhood as a construct. It is now widely accepted that human impacts on the Earth are so extensive and pervasive that modernity's conception of nature, as other to the human world, has become untenable. This argument proposes that we live in the Anthropocene where the human and natural world are so completely entangled that not only is any return to a pristine, pre-human wilderness unimaginable, but that distinctions between the human and natural worlds are meaningless (Bonneuil and Fressoz, 2015; Blundell, 2017; Lewis and Maslin, 2018). For ecological philosopher Tim Morton (2010, 2018), this demands a broader understanding, wherein economic phenomena and human interests are recognised as component parts alongside many others in an ecological 'mesh' that embraces the living and non-living fabric of planet Earth. It encourages us to understand economic phenomena in terms of their extensive ecological impacts through the mesh. This applies to the past and questions surrounding how we got to be where we are, so that *economic history* should more helpfully be re-imagined as a series of *ecological histories* that examine how humans have placed themselves in relation to the planet as well as the impacts that these standpoints facilitated (Dukes, 2011).

In August 2018 a 15-year-old school student, Greta Thunberg, skipped lessons and sat outside the Swedish parliament building in Stockholm with a home-made banner as a solitary protest against inaction surrounding climate change. On Friday 15 March 2019 hundreds of thousands of children and young people joined her *skolstrejk för klimatet* (school strike for climate) in over 700 locations across 71 countries arguing that schooling that ignored this most pressing issue was pointless (Watts, 2019). Subsequently, Thunberg was lauded by the UN, met the French president, shared a platform with the president of the European Commission, and was endorsed by Angela

Merkel, the German chancellor. Normative beliefs are inverted when those who are assumed to be subordinate in their capacity to understand by virtue of age or development challenge the presumptions of schooling and its institutional logic of 'adult world knows best'. Greta Thunberg and the climate strikers live the reality of the Anthropocene and recognise that the impacts of global warming change everything at a quite fundamental level. Their youthfulness serves to challenge demarcations between future, past and present that underpin the sapiential authority claimed by schooling; rather, the climate strikers emphasise their entanglement and that the trope of futurity as endless linear progress stretching far into the distance has been overtaken by a pressing need to cooperate with the Earth as a finite entity.

Armed with the Anthropocene proposition and from the standpoint of the twenty-first century it seems timely to re-interpret the economic history of childhood presented earlier more usefully as one component of an ecological history and thereby to ask how the naturalisation of childhood has facilitated schooling and institutional practices predicated on children as incipient human capital. It would be crass to suggest that in the immediate term this recognition can in itself achieve the necessary transformation in economic justice that will ease the challenges Mary and children like her face. However, denaturalising childhood can invite a greater interest in the actuality of children's lives and work (including the demands of schooling) as well as affording them the same entitlement to be heard and listened to in matters concerning their lives as for others. Steps have been taken in this direction with the appearance of the UNCRC and the NSSC. The challenge of climate change is grave and will make comprehensive demands on all existing institutions. If the worst outcomes are to be avoided responses must not only be concerned with how humans interact with non-humans or even, the more-than-human 'mesh' but also how humans live with and value each other. All of which has vital implications for education and the responsibilities of educators as we face the next 150 years.

Questions for reflection

1. Can children's work or labour and schooling be reconciled and what implications might this have for the latter?
2. What do you think education and childhood might look like by the end of the twenty-first century?

Summary points

- The chapter opens by outlining the conditions surrounding the introduction of the 1870 Elementary Education Act a century and a half ago and explores the impact of universal schooling in reconstructing commonplace attitudes to childhood and the place of children. Amongst these was a deferral of children's direct contribution to economic activity through work or labour.
- Amongst the most contentious areas to emerge from this reconstruction surrounded children's work/labour, family income and economy and their attendance at school.
- The chapter examines work/labour and schooling in the contemporary world and suggests that we need to know more about the actuality of children's lives and include them in the discussions.

- The chapter closes by suggesting that constructions of nature inherited from Enlightenment modernity are fundamentally challenged by climate change and the advent of the Anthropocene. Relations between the human and non-human worlds are radically re-cast as profoundly entangled and enmeshed, thereby inviting a denaturalisation of childhood that challenges many institutional assumptions surrounding schooling and its practices.

Recommended readings

Blundell, D. (2017) 'Nature', childhood, and the Anthropocene: evaluating the challenges for Education Studies. *Educational Futures*, 8(1), pp. 3–18.
Hendrick, H. (1997) *Children, Childhood and English Society 1880–1990*. Cambridge: Cambridge University Press.
Lewis, S.L. and Maslin, M.A. (2018) *The Human Planet: How We Created the Anthropocene*. London: Pelican.
Morton, T. (2018) *Being Ecological*. London: Pelican.
Taylor, A. (2013) *Reconfiguring the Natures of Childhood*. Abingdon: Routledge.

References

Aitken, S., Lund, R. and Kjørholt, A.T. (2007) Why children? Why now? *Children's Geographies*, 5(1–2), pp. 3–14.
Blundell, D. (2012) *Education and Constructions of Childhood*. London and New York: Continuum.
Blundell, D. (2017) 'Nature', childhood, and the Anthropocene: evaluating the challenges for Education Studies. *Educational Futures*, 8(1), pp. 3–18.
Blundell, D. (forthcoming) Education, urbanisation and the case of 'the child in the city'. In C.A. Simon and G. Downes (eds.), *Sociology for Education Studies: Connecting Theory, Settings and Everyday Experiences*. Abingdon: Routledge.
Bonneuil, C. and Fressoz, J.-B. (2015) *The Shock of the Anthropocene: The Earth, History and Us*. London: Verso.
Briggs, A. (1991) *The Collected Essays of Asa Briggs, Vol. III – Serious Pursuits: Communications and Education*. London: Harvester Wheatsheaf.
Cunningham, H. (2006) *The Invention of Childhood*. London: BBC Books.
Dickinson, C.M. (1889). *The Children, and Other Verses*. New York: Cassell.
Diptee, A.A. (2007) Imperial ideas, colonial realities: enslaved children in Jamaica, 1775–1834. In J. Marten (ed.), *Children in Colonial America*. New York: New York University Press.
Dukes, P. (2011) *Minutes to Midnight: History and the Anthropocene Era from 1763*. London: Anthem Press.
Earle, J. (1628) *Microcosmographie, or, A Peece of the World Discovered in Essayes and Characters*. Available at: https://books.google.co.uk/books/about/Micro_cosmographie.html?id=uWQUAQAAMAAJ&printsec=frontcover&source=kp_read_button&redir_esc=y#v=onepage&q&f=false (Accessed 23 May 2019).
Hansard, HC Deb 17 February 1870 vol. 199 cc438-98. Available at: https://api.parliament.uk/historic-hansard/commons /1870/feb/17/leave-first-reading (Accessed 9 April 2019).
Hendrick, H. (1997) *Children, Childhood and English Society 1880–1990*. Cambridge: Cambridge University Press.
Hendrick, H. (2015) Constructions and reconstructions of British childhood: an interpretive survey, 1800 to the present. In A. James and A. Prout (eds.), *Constructing and Reconstructing Childhood: Contemporary Issues in the Sociological Study of Childhood*. Abingdon: Routledge.
Horn, P. (1994) *Children's Work and Welfare, 1780–1890*. Cambridge: Cambridge University Press.
James, A. and Prout, A. (eds.) (1990) *Constructing and Reconstructing Childhood: Contemporary Issues in the Sociological Study of Childhood* (1st edition). London: Routledge.
Kjørholt, A.T. (2007) Childhood as a symbolic space: searching for authentic voices in the era of globalisation. *Children's Geographies*, 5(1–2), pp. 29–42.
Lewis, S.L. and Maslin, M.A. (2018) *The Human Planet: How We Created the Anthropocene*. London: Pelican.
Morton, T. (2010) *The Ecological Thought*. Cambridge, MA: Harvard University Press.
Morton, T. (2018) *Being Ecological*. London: Pelican.
Pratt-Adams, S., Maguire, M. and Burn, E. (2010) *Changing Urban Education: Contemporary Issues in Education Studies*. London: Continuum.
Taylor, A. (2013) *Reconfiguring the Natures of Childhood*. London: Routledge.

United Nations (1989) *United Nations Convention on the Rights of the Child* Available at: www.unicef.org/crc/ (Accessed 22 May 2019).

United Nations Development Programme (2015) Millennium Development Goals. Available at: www.undp.org/content/undp/en/home/sdgoverview/mdg_goals.html (Accessed 22 May 2019).

United Nations Development Programme (2015) Sustainable Development Goals. Available at: https://sustainabledevelopment.un.org/?menu=1300 (Accessed 22 May 2019).

Watts, J. (2019) Greta Thunberg, schoolgirl climate change warrior: 'Some people can let things go. I can't'. *The Guardian*, 11 March 2019. Available at: www.theguardian.com/world/2019/mar/11/greta-thunberg-schoolgirl-climate-change-warrior-some-people-can-let-things-go-i-cant (Accessed May 2019).

Wells, K. (2009) *Childhood in a Global Perspective*. London: Polity.

Zelizer, V. (1994) *Pricing the Priceless Child: The Changing Social Value of Children.* Princeton, NJ: Princeton University Press.

4 Authority and trust beyond neoliberalism
A critical reflection on education as useful for the economy

Eleonora Pedron

Introduction

This chapter analyses the way in which neoliberalism threatens educational authority and the ties of trust that sustain it. It proposes a series of reflections designed to invite the development of new educational theory and pedagogical experience. The chapter offers a critical reflection on the obstacles to authority within education in a society that is dominated by neoliberal values and expectations. Neoliberalism attempts to put education at the service of the economy, directing it towards performance and competitiveness, for the formation of human resources for capitalism. It can be argued that utilitarianism and competition degrade human relationships, which end up playing on the level of power rather than on the level of authority, the latter perceived as constraining. Because every person is different and people constantly change through experiences, education must recognise and respect this, becoming capable of adapting and responding to individual peculiarities. This requires a balance in order not to fall into relativism. Education cannot be based solely on criteria of measurability and standardisation that seem to characterise a dominant narrative, linked to employment markets and to the development of skills deemed 'economically useful'. Rather, it is proposed that education should accommodate/foster/enable paths that are not necessarily determined by measured results, both because people in a becoming stage cannot always understand and determine their goals, and because educational paths are, by definition, complex and unpredictable in their results.

The chapter pays particular attention to the ideology of 'utility', which invites both educators and the educated to invest in the educational process only when there is a specific purpose, seen in terms of material or symbolic gain. The ideology of utility clashes with the model of educational authority that demands continuous acts of trust, even when the ultimate goal of this process is not understood. In this context, I refer to my research and work experience within schools and with families. I present some case studies to support my proposals. I also refer to the works of Diotima, a women's philosophical community centred on the University of Verona since 1983. This community is one of the most important references for Feminist thinking about Sexual Difference, together with the *Libreria delle Donne di Milano*. My engagement with Feminist theory and theorists, and this community in particular, has offered me alternatives to the dominant representations of the world, as well as alternative pedagogies. The 'Feminism of Difference' recognises the complexity of human beings starting from the first and basic human difference: the difference between men and women, demonstrating that dominant discourses and representations are presented as neutral when they are in fact male. I refer to this theoretical perspective and work because it shapes reality creatively, above and beyond the given order. Highlighting differences between different world views, 'Feminism of Difference' has also brought with it a new pedagogy (Piussi, 1990) seeking alternative narratives from that of neoliberalism which emerges from a male perspective and proposes an ancient logic of power and control where relationships are based on utilitarianism and individualism. The chapter uses this concept to problematise the neoliberal values and approaches which have been seeping into in education. Especially through the studies of Diotima it is possible to recognise that these authority-based ideas are founded upon a rigid and hierarchical asymmetry, originating from a constantly-renewed reformulation of trust rooted in specific experience. The aim of the chapter is to highlight the possibility of reconfiguring authority and trust to achieve a fairer education, with an education system that goes above and beyond neoliberalist ideas.

Authority and trust: traces of meaning

Before analysing the intersection between education and economics in the field of authority, I should clarify what I mean by 'authority' and stress its links to the concept of trust. Broadly speaking, authority means the power or right to give orders, make decisions, and enforce obedience. The feminist philosopher Luisa Muraro identifies the difficulty of this definition, and of using the term 'authority', especially in the contemporary West. According to Muraro (2013), the term is problematic because it is too readily linked to political power, oppression and abuse. Moreover, within neoliberal Western society an emphasis on (supposed) individual freedom makes people wary of the very idea of authority. With a focus on individual autonomy and the pursuit of success, authority is often interpreted as limiting one's own growth path.

In education it is undoubtedly important to strengthen the autonomy of young people, but today we are witnessing an exaggerated drive towards autonomy, even in education. This can become an avoidance of authority among adults and an excessive burden of responsibility for young people. In this case adult responsibilities are delegated to children. In the name of autonomy and free self-expression, adults too often ask children to choose for themselves: from what they want for supper, to decisions about their education. Too many choices can generate anxiety, imposing responsibility that young people are not yet able to sustain. This responsibility should be part of the authority, which should be *entrusted* to adults.

From a commonsense perspective, this leads to a false dilemma: the choice between confusion of '*at least there is freedom!*' and the risk of slipping into the abuse of authority ('*at least we won't get lost!*') (Muraro, 2013: 24). However, whoever proposes this choice is actually confusing authority with authoritarianism, where the former corrupts the latter through abuse of power. Authority is always relational (Bingham, 2009), a person or institution has authority when it is conferred; for authority to exist it needs to be recognised by others; authority is neither stable nor final. In this sense, authority permits freedom because its essence and its origin are relational. Trust is, therefore, intertwined with authority: the second cannot exist without the first; but even cultivating a feeling of trust is difficult if there is no authority in the relationship. Authoritarianism, by contrast, stems not from a trusting act of conferment, but from abuse of power, an abusing physical or symbolic force to ensure that disparity is maintained, even when it is not – or is no longer – beneficial.

What then is authority? Authority is neither rational nor irrational (Muraro, 2013) and depends on the subjective aspects of who stands in that specific relationship. The attribution of authority always maintains a degree of rational inexplicability. We can never fully articulate it with a vocabulary of rationality. It is also for this reason that the positivist vocabulary of neoliberalism, which aims at the standardisation of differences, struggles to depict the need for authority rather than authoritarianism. Education cannot be imposed from above but must be respectful of the relationship between teachers and students; however, that does not provide a level playing field between educator and learner. Instead, it can be argued that, in order to better realise the specific qualities of each person, the guidance from someone more experienced is needed: an expert guide – the adult – who is able to take on responsibilities and who recognises when these responsibilities can be – gradually – entrusted to the person in training.

Although it is distinct from power (Diotima, 1995), authority has an inner force which is mostly symbolic. In the context of educational relationships, authority has a symbolic and practical energy which is not exercised *over* the other person, but is brought into play *in favour* of those who rely on the educator.

> [W]e feel it when it is recognised within us and when we recognise it in others; we feel it as strength, responsibility, reverence, trembling but also tranquility and reassurance or, again, as an urge to act and a widening of our possibilities … in English they have a name, *trust*, and a verb, *to trust*, which summarise well the feelings that accompany authority.
> (Muraro, 2013: 49, author's translation)

The symbolic and practical energy of authority reflects that the greater experience of the educator offers the opportunity to guide the other, but not solely: once the other chooses to *trust* the educator, the latter puts his/her entire experience and existential position at the disposal of the educated. If the educator brings authority into play, even her/his presence becomes educational: s/he can lead by example as well as teaching. It is important that the educator is aware of this: once s/he assumes – and is entrusted with – authority, s/he becomes one of the models that the person who is learning chooses as a mirror as they build their own identity.

Authority is thus closely linked to trust. Authority is not abusive when it embodies its original meaning relying on trust, when it eschews abuse of power and rigidity, and when it accepts change. Authority actually promotes change: it fosters personal growth when it is free to transform itself in harmony with the transformation of the relationship as a dynamic process of growth. Mediation, not imposition, is the cardinal concept of authority. Mediation takes place when the educator assumes the authority to adapt pedagogy manuals, ministerial guidelines, expert instructions, and her/his own certainties, to the uniqueness of the people s/he is educating. This ability enables a critical dialogue with the policies imposed on education by neoliberalism. Asking for standardised assessments, targets, measures, benchmarks, and employment market-oriented curricula, neoliberal policies reduce education to the manipulation of people to serve economic demands. Education should instead be a maieutical process to enable the better realisation of everyone's potential. For this reason educators must assume authority to distance education from neoliberal ideology and return to enriched educational practice.

The main way of effecting authority is through the practice of mediation. The person invested with authority carries out a continuous work of mediation in favour of the other: a mediation between the educated and the rest of the world. The educator's task is making the world and the relationships attainable, but as a main task s/he has also to be capable of an inner mediation, *to be* attainable.

This is what allows the relationship of authority to be generative, to open the present and the self to the inherent possibilities.

Mediation is therefore the main element that distinguishes authority from power. Power

> is a formidable abbreviation; exonerates us from the effort of mediation. ... In an order in which the balance of power is worth, those who prevail with their power ... do not feel the need to create common places in which to bargain to live freely.
>
> (Muraro, 2013: 57–58, author's translation)

As pointed out, in contrast, authority stresses growth (the Latin *auctoritas* derives from *augere*, to increase). However, in educational terms, growth should not be seen as a growth of goods and services and an increase in profits as it is in economics, but rather in terms of the promotion and development of the potential of individuals. Authority, then, represents a relationship in which those who are being educated rely upon the greater experience of the educator, an experience that the latter offers within a relationship of growth. In this process, not only do those being educated grow, but those educating also have the opportunity to transform.

Authority does not mean that the educator never makes mistakes and never doubts her/his experience and knowledge: it is her/his responsibility to question and to review them in the light of the uniqueness of the other. Contrary to neoliberal aspirations, because all relationships are different and dynamic, uncertainty cannot be eliminated. A true authority movement presupposes that educators take responsibility for their decision to lead the other in a specific direction. We assist authority when adults (educators) take a leading position, but can admit their mistakes when the outcomes are not those desired. Authority confirms itself in the moment in which it admits its own limitation and its own errors: accepting that authority 'is fragile, is the antidote to all idolatry. ... Authority is ... a fragile factor that orients the search for answers, with the extraordinary advantage that, in order to act, it cannot renounce our freedom' (Muraro, 2013: 106, author's translation). Authority, therefore, can only express itself in the presence of trust and, at the same time, it generates trust in those who are in a relationship with it.

Questions for reflection

1. What is the difference between authority and power?
2. Based on the difference you identified between authority and power, can you think of examples in which you experienced either in education?
3. What role does trust play within the process of education?

Between utility and trust: the dialectic between neoliberal values and authority in education

Today there is widespread talk of a crisis of authority, not only in academia but also in everyday life. Referring to the socio-cultural and economic conditions of the globalised north-western world, the adult population (parents-teachers), but, more generally, society as a broader educational agency, seems in a state of aporia. Existence has become unpredictable, precarious and disrupted in the face of rapid social change, postmodernity and globalisation; the exponential development of technologies and accelerated capitalism seem to have escaped human agency to become virtual and dominates all spheres of life (Bauman, 2000; Beck, 2000; Giddens, 1990). Underpinning this is a valorisation of, and demand for, flexibility which, starting from the economy of flexible capital, comes to involve every aspect of human existence. The demand for flexibility has penetrated everyday life, changed relationships and shaped ideals and plans. This affects the way we educate. If everything is precarious, how can we build our own future or help to build the future of those who rely on us? What are the goals we strive for? Will they still be valid when we attain them? What values can we rely on in a society that changes so rapidly?

Difference Feminism with its pedagogy identifies alternative and creative ways of looking at the present, without minimising genuine challenges:

> resisting the established order, though a resistance based on creation and opening new possibilities, and, thus, genuinely emancipatory, rather than an opposition based on hand-to-hand combat with the present reality: which latter, in addition to being logically and symbolically dependent on what it denies, sustains itself from forces of reaction and resentment, rather than releasing positive energies. It is from this perspective that we should rethink a 'pedagogy of resistance' in the contemporary landscape.
>
> (Piussi, 2008: note 17, p. 34, author's translation)

In Italy, some primary school teachers (see especially Mecenero, 2004; Cosentino et al., 2008), drawing on Feminism of Difference, have been able to enhance an awareness of everyday teaching practices and the nurturing of significant relationships with other teachers helps preserve individual authority to remain faithful to the original values that guided the personal choice of becoming a teacher. Teachers can return to enjoying, rather than surviving, school.

Regaining authority is thus one of the first commitments required to allow for transformation and growth. This observation is primarily valid for those who deal with education. However, society today does not make this task easy. A principal obstacle to authority and trust is the culture that neoliberalism has spread so widely and penetrated deeply school and family life. A commercially driven logic has moved from the economic sphere to places commonly thought of as distinct or private. One of the noticeable effects of this neoliberal ideology is the need for teachers to constantly adapt to changing curricula, changing pedagogy which undermines not just their expertise but also their authority. Neoliberalism in schools has meant that the experience and subject knowledge of teachers becomes a secondary priority in a world where curricula are increasingly shaped by the needs of industry and the changing economy instead of the needs of educators and pupils or school communities.

In the following section, I highlight different ways in which profit, as the main value of neoliberalism, subverts the educational authority of parents and teachers.

The school's performance management and the passivisation of teachers

The leadership that neoliberalism imposes contributes to the difficulties currently experienced in the world of education (Benasayag and Schmit, 2004; Piussi 2011, 2012). Neoliberalism requires standardised, fast, and quantifiable assessment and teaching procedures in line with the dominant corporate and commercial vision of individual and collective living (Nussbaum, 2010). In Europe and North America from primary school to university, educational institutions are increasingly adopting the traits of businesses; students are treated as customers; educational curricula are shaped by market logic.

In Italy, the terminology recently adopted to define aspects of daily school life is an indication of this tendency. The trend is towards developing *skills*, recognising and reproducing *good practices* as if they were algorithms regardless of the difference of every educational context. Difficulties become *formative debts*. Learning is acquired through *credits*. For some years head teachers have been called *dirigenti*, corresponding to *executives*. This neoliberal drift occurs in the United Kingdom too: Stephen Ball (2003, 2016) explains how the management of performance seeps through school and undermines teachers' professionalism and threatens education. What Ball calls 'professionalism' is actually teachers' authority. Bending to market logic, education loses its original sense and teachers see their role reduced to having to apply the demands of rapidly-changing educational policy and an economic system. If students are seen as customers, they will feel like customers, expecting the teacher to be at their service instead of trusting their expert guide.

Simultaneously, and counter to neoliberal orientations, those involved in education receive from the pedagogical literature and certain national and supranational policies an impulse towards educational action that recognises, enhances, and develops the peculiarities of the individual. If this important orientation towards diversity is central to the pedagogical discourse, it nevertheless tends to be conveyed by the so-called experts: organisms and subjects mostly far from the direct experience of everyday school life, who send their indications from academies and government institutions. This distance and separation mean that teachers must negotiate contradictory indications – on the one hand, the request for personalisation to meet the needs of each student; on the other, the request for standard and measurable study paths – that are mostly inapplicable to the real classes they deal with.

Yet neither neoliberal orientations nor more ethical person-centred guidelines are readily applicable in the overcrowded classroom of the vast majority of schools. Considering also the constant pressures on resources, it is increasingly difficult to offer support to individual teachers by, for example, their working alongside other professionals (Lascioli, 2014). The demands that the ministries and literature make on the teaching profession are unsustainable when the neoliberal system stresses productivity and the training towards *human capital*. These numerous and heterogeneous directives are likely to undermine teachers' authority, leaving little energy and time to devote to their educational vocation. Excessive guidelines on how teachers should act, combined with workload fatigue, are likely to make them regret choosing their profession, even though they have developed and refined their work through study and professional experience. If the teachers themselves no longer have faith in what they are doing, it becomes impossible to build a relationship of trust and authority with pupils.

The most decisive attack on the authority of teachers is the passivisation they undergo when faced with the demands of institutions that make decisions for the school without experiencing its everyday life:

> Sweep us away, sweep us away as they do in university research, as they call it, although it is really always training, because we have always to be trained. We have no structure; sometimes, it seems as though we can have one, but rapidly we realise that we remain insufficiently defined;

prepare guides for us, guides of all kinds; there is no end to this need to direct us, to shepherd us with instructions, with well-defined actions to follow step by step.

(Mecenero, 2004: 10, author's translation)

The teacher's professional role is thus increasingly reduced to that of implementing orders from higher and external bodies. The media have also strengthened the social control of schools and teachers: productivity, effectiveness, and usefulness of teaching are constantly monitored not only by institutions, but also by parents and students – and the wider public.

Information about schools is harvested in ways that rarely make provision for genuine involvement from teachers. There are numerous reports and research which disseminate news on education; scholastic programmes and standardised assessment systems allow scientific bodies to carry out comprehensive statistics and studies; experts debate the state of the school system in different countries or at a supranational level. Studies of the real experience of everyday life in schools are rare: in Italy, Maria Cristina Mecenero (2004) and Vita Cosentino and Marina Santini (2008); in Spain José Contreras Domingo (2010) and Josè Contreras Domingo and Nuria Pérez De Lara (2016); in the United Kingdom, Gert J.J. Biesta, Mark Priestley and Sarah Robinson (2015, 2017); in the United States, D. Jean Clandinin and F. Michael Connelly (1988) have recognised the value of teachers' experience, and the importance, as well as the urgency, of giving them a voice. These scholars have, in short, recognised the authority of teachers.

However, giving voice to the teachers and considering their real experiences is not only a recognition of authority by the scholars and by those who use their findings. Qualitative and participatory research approaches, related to the phenomenological epistemology, enable teachers to be protagonists in the heuristic process, becoming researchers themselves instead of being passivised as subjects of interest. The research thus can become an opportunity for teaching staff to foster awareness of their own knowledge and emotions. Recognition of their authority and experience from outside the school also helps teachers to perceive and develop a sense of their own authority, to rediscover the value of their *being-there*, and to signify their own agency. Enhancing and disseminating a school culture originating in actual experience could also help to challenge the neoliberal control of educational curricula which requires a passive posture from and towards teachers, and stifling the pedagogical intent of educational pathways of sacrifice at the altar of neoliberalism.

In my professional and research experience in the daily reality of educational contexts, I have been able to observe how the teachings and indications received from the outside, as well as the operative strategies suggested to the teachers, are often difficult to accept and implement. Their validity is expressed only when such tools are allowed to interact and change in relation to other forms of knowledge, those less visible and not yet valorised: the ingredients of teachers' authority that constitute the vital component of educational practice and pedagogical knowledge. It is, therefore, worth restoring authority to teachers by asking them to express their knowledge originating from experience; scientific and political bodies need to listen to teachers' perspectives and build on them. Only in this way is it possible to implement policies that are valid and pedagogically fruitful.

Beyond utilitarianism: recover authority with trust

Authority does not impose itself from above; it does not even come from above. Trust and authority, as Difference Feminism suggests, must be sought out and built *starting from oneself*: they cannot be found outside. When adult educators complain about the crisis of authority, they are ignoring their responsibility: it is first of all in themselves that they must be committed to finding it.

What follows is a brief case study from my research and professional experience. It exemplifies the link between authority and trust and how, despite neoliberal threats, it can transcend them.

I was recently asked to perform a task in an unusual field for me as a pedagogist and trainer. A group of Christian catechists approached me to support them in working with children and young people. For me this was a new environment, a novel subject. My value was as an outsider. The catechists wanted help in negotiating their relationship with their pupils; my experience with children and adolescents inside and outside school offered a different perspective when those catechising no longer knew what kind of strategies to adopt. The problem they expressed was that the children no longer listened to them. This had two major practical implications: the confusing and disrespectful behaviour of those being catechised, and the difficulty of leading children along the path of the catechism, of accompanying them in their journey of faith. The situation of these catechists was similar to those I had encountered among many teachers; only the content of the teaching differed.

I mention this experience because it emphasises the issue of authority in the educational field, where the risk is following educational paths only when they are useful, and this usefulness is measured only in economic terms, where the gain is already predictable, tangible and measurable. This brief case study highlights the role of authority since the path of faith requires perfect trust: the exact opposite of what utilitarianism demands. Within a framework such as teaching the catechism, the concept of faith and authority are understood in a meaning closest to the archetypal. Yet they simultaneously demand a willingness to interact with a level of abstraction with which we are unaccustomed because of the pragmatic and rational outlook adopted in everyday life. The catechists, like every educating adult, faced a problem of authority when teaching. But there was another broader issue of authority: in the religious field, young people are invited to develop faith, a faith in words and teachings, but also a faith in the original source of such words and teachings. This faith, by definition, cannot be founded on proofs or motivations, rational or pragmatic.

The reflection I proposed to the catechists concerned authority. I started from the analysis of the context in which new generations are growing in industrialised countries, where neoliberalism – far from being just an economic philosophy – has become a hegemonic culture to which children are exposed from their very earliest encounters with the education system. The principle of profit becomes part of every choice, replacing the desire of adults, but even more of the young people who are bombarded with messages of fear and uncertainty, led to believe that the only way to exist is through competition, fending for themselves (Benasayag and Schmit, 2004), adopting strategies and choices that sustain individual survival. This neoliberal narrative tells us that we are increasingly precarious, that the previous generation's promises for the future turned out to be lies, that nothing is certain, not even science; we are experiencing the failure of positivism, of science and of industrialism as tickets to the future. In order to survive it is necessary to invest in oneself, to develop flexibility, to adapt to the fluctuations of the all-powerful market, always trying to keep a slice for oneself, aspiring only to individual and financial success.

These social premises explain, partly at least, why educational relations between adults and young people have been transformed into peer relationships, lacking the almost guaranteed asymmetry of the past. Neoliberal ideology also underpins the attitude, widespread among adults in education, that they need to explain to their pupils the reasons and purposes of everything they teach. This reflects the neoliberal need to justify everything with usefulness, to find possible gain in every action undertaken. The attempt to provide almost material justifications for every bit of an educational programme seems to offer security, to offer some certainty when faced by an uncertain future. In this way adults are rejecting their own security, their authority, by justifying their actions and choices in terms of external benefits. In doing so they also discard educational asymmetry. Children and young people now assume the responsibility that once belonged to parents or teachers. Young people must evaluate choices without recourse to adults. Such dynamics are linked to an affective need of adults who seem to have ever greater difficulty in accepting the possibility of conflict with their children. A consequence is that the family that has gone from being *ethical* – based on rules, limits, parental authority – to *emotional*, where adults seek agreement with their children (and where the latter lack boundaries to break during adolescence) (Pietropolli Charmet, 2000). Conceiving the educational process in terms of an illusory certainty of outcome protects from the possibility of failure and especially from the anguish of participating in a process where the results are not controllable. Adults prefer to delegate responsibility because they cannot offer future certainty, which in turn engenders uncertainty about authority.

The issue with utility

Teachers start from a disadvantaged position when it comes to having their authority recognised. The social system does not ensure them opportunities. The prevailing human model transmitted by the media and internalised by pupils is very different from that embraced by most teachers, who have usually studied and worked very hard to pursue a vocation that does not offer the sort of economic rewards or sorts of personal success that the younger generation have internalised from the media (Benasayag and Schmit, 2004). This is evident from students' questions at school, which reveal the degree to which they accept the logic of profit: subjects become interesting when teachers can explain objectives in terms of concrete gains; teachers are role models when they reflect material success. Many times I have heard students ask teachers, 'How much are you paid?', 'What is the point of studying this subject?', 'What car do you drive?', 'What smartphone do you own?', 'Why should I study as you did, and then earn so little?'

These questions are rooted in utilitarianism but must also be recognised as a way for pupils to test, even to challenge, the authority of adults. In fact, they can be reconsidered as requests addressed to the adult to be an example for young people, to witness her/his way to live in the world.

These questions can be frightening for teachers: they can put them in the situation of not knowing how to answer, fearing that they might trigger a conflict with pupils; or they can generate a sense of defeat and the impossibility of dialogue with the younger generations. These thoughts and feelings, however, close any possibility of educating. Educating means providing, through one's own example, experience and knowledge, an additional alternative: one more possibility for those who are being educated to build their own identity and their own life path. If we consider that every person is constantly evolving, we must never lose the confidence of being able to offer new possibilities for growth.

Different visions, different attributions of meaning, necessarily come into conflict. In this sense, conflict should not be feared; rather it should be rethought as an opportunity for transformation for those involved. Instead of resolving differences by denying them and denying conflict, or worse still imposing meanings through recourse to power, it is necessary to engage in confrontation and dialogue. Without falling into a relationship between peers, without the adults denying their authority by delegating their own responsibilities, involving students in dialogic practices helps them also to develop critical thinking and to open their vision to different possibilities. Educators, with their authority, must guide the confrontation without losing trust in themselves and in the other. This demands assuming responsibility and remaining stable – solid but not rigid – in the face of uncertainty, looking for new creative possibilities that start from a relationship beyond market forces. This would foster within schools an environment in which teachers and pupils allow authority to circulate, taking advantage of varied perspectives to enrich the educational experience of younger generations.

To be guides and authorities, teachers must educate to trust. School is first and foremost a place where to learn how to live. It is important to enhance those practices and those teachings that do not have an immediate response, the ones that it is not possible immediately to perceive that they yield a concrete gain. These lessons can train how to stay in the present and, at the same time, to be able to wait indefinitely to gather the results of efforts. The very stages of growth, of life, do not have precise times. Is this not the essence of education? It responds to the complexity of every single person and to their dynamism, which is why education itself cannot predict precisely which goals and when they will be achieved. Whoever deals with education knows and experiences every day the unpredictability of educational contexts and of the people who inhabit them. Educators are accustomed to seeing their goals change during the journey to adapt them to people as they change. They know that sometimes they will not be able to see the results of their work because what is sown in education may blossom in the distant future. Educational practice is therefore supported by trust, so why not teach it?

It is worthwhile rethinking the paradigm of the current world to see its possibilities. Life itself is unpredictable and ontologically precarious. The scenario of the current world and its precariousness do not thus teach us anything new, but perhaps emphasise what already belongs to our existence.

The educators, the teachers, with their authority, can therefore be mediators of living, of the *being in the world*: through the trust that they instil in their students; they can show that trust can be placed in the relationships that occur in education and schools.

Questions for reflection

1. How can conflict as a comparison of differences promote trust and authority in relationships?
2. Which practices and which spaces can help educators and teachers to recover the profound meaning of their authority?

Conclusion

Authority and trust: an alternative to a market-logic-oriented education

Let me return to the catechists. How was it possible for them to ask young people to listen to words and teachings that had no obvious utility, which did not yield immediately in demonstrable results, which did not fully explain the reason for their invitations? How was it possible for them to teach the faith in its original sense, that is to place one's trust in something without knowing in advance what the gains would be, gains for which there is no earthly, material, rational, sure proof? The problem faced by the catechists was not different from that of other educators. All educators require a transcendent, otherworldly, literally immaterial authority.

Authority deals with the affective and symbolic sphere, which is impalpable; moreover, it does not always explain the reasons and the usefulness of the directions it gives. Precisely for this reason it allows the differences to be appreciated and the different roles of a relationship to be respected, leaving everyone their own responsibilities.

> 'Why did you stop?' I replied: 'Because you aren't doing what I ordered.' And I added: 'Look, we're not on television where a person spends a quarter of an hour explaining to the child why he has to obey, when he already knows.' He laughed: he had understood and was fine. What was there to understand? The possibility to switch from a gruelling trial of strength where you could submit or prevail, to a relationship that guaranteed him, without pretence, his dignity as a child.
> (Muraro, 2013: 38, author's translation)

It is, therefore, the responsibility of adults to ensure both their own welfare and that of children by assuming authority and educating in authority. Authority is a gift from the educator, an act of responsibility towards the other. Responsibility derives from the latin *respòndere*, to respond; authority derives from *auctor*, author: what is expected from an adult if not primarily that s/he knows how to account for her/his actions, to respond as an author?

Knowing how to respond to what we do, and what we express, demands a readiness to observe and work on ourselves in order to respond to the questions and the call from someone else. It means being able to support the difficult act of observing and questioning ourselves, of not shying away from conflict with children and pupils. In this sense authority is what permits the creation of order in relationships, both in the adult-child relationship and in that between different educating adults, between parents and teachers. It allows access to an order of relationships distinct from that based on profit or utility.

Authority offers us the best antidote to authoritarianism and to neoliberal ideology: it allows education to distance itself from the need for utilitarian legitimacy because it responds to a need that is not material but symbolic (Muraro, 2013: 107), without the need to replace these justifications through coercion. Young people seem to accept only these alternatives: the temptation of neoliberalism or coercive imposition.

> [T]he mere idea of saying 'You must listen and respect me simply because I am responsible for this relationship' now seems inadmissible. In the name of alleged individual liberty, the student or the young person takes on the role of client who accepts or rejects what the 'adult-seller' proposes to them. And when this strategy fails, there is no other way out than that recourse to coercion. ... These two temptations are actually nothing but two of the variants of authoritarianism inevitably provoked by the symmetrical relationship between young people and adults.
> (Benasayag and Schmit, 2004: 27, author's translation)

Authority values the whole relationship, enhances those who embody it, but also those who recognise it. Authority does not have a foundation; authority *is* a foundation (Muraro, 2013: 36), one shared by both parties within the relationship. It is, indeed, unequal: one party leads and the other follows; but at the same time it is a relationship endowed with something that is above both, a common principle on which that specific relationship – 'which wants to free itself from dependence or rebelliousness generated by power relations but also by the symbolic sterility of peer relationships' (Muraro, 2013: 54) – is founded.

Without guaranteeing anything material, the educational relationship of authority commits itself to valorise a disparity in order to realise a relationship of exchange and transformation. In a world driven by neoliberalism and its principles of utility and competition, it seems difficult to cherish a true form of education based on trust. Yet it is precisely in these times that it is essential for adults to be witnesses to a form of education that places people at its core, rather than the dictates of the neoliberal system. Only in this way is it possible to renew the profoundly human aspect of educational relationships and teaching, and to fulfil the delicate process of passing the baton to the younger generations.

The quality of our being in the world depends on relationships. The ability to live in the complexity and uncertainty of the current world, overcoming the tendency towards closure and fear; the possibility of living life with curiosity, trust and desire – avoiding competition, individualism and the commodification of relationships and paths of life – depends on the quality of the answers we receive and the questions we learn to ask on our existential journey.

Recognising the need for authority means recognising the need for these questions and answers, accepting the human constitutive vulnerability, valuing the difference as a generative dimension and the relationship as a creative force. It means recognising education as an alternative to the neoliberal drift of individual and collective life.

Summary points

- Neoliberalism, combined with a common sense of uncertainty about the future, is undermining education at many levels from its cardinal elements: authority and trust. These are especially threatened by a pervasive utilitarian direction of educational relationships and choices.
- Authority is at the very basis of the educational relationship: adult responsibility to accompany the other in her/his own growth path. Authority is different from power and authoritarianism, because it requires and generates trust to exist. Authority, therefore, operates on a different level from that of neoliberalism, taking care and enhancing differences and requiring trust to exist: trust in relationships and paths where the results are neither certain nor quantifiable.
- At school, the demands imposed from above and the pressures of neoliberalism risk undermining teachers' trust, hence their authority and ability to generate trust in their students. At home, facing a perception of uncertainty about the future and the desire for success for their children, parents risk limiting their own authority, excessively charging their children with responsibility. Overprotectiveness is often a compensation that generates conflict with teachers.
- Authority is an alternative to both neoliberal and coercive narrative in education. Parents and teachers have the task of assuming authority building relationships of trust beyond the challenges of neoliberal utilitarianism. This is possible through self-awareness, mutual recognition and alliance between educating adults, the ability to mediate and question knowledges and experiences to make education attentive to individual difference.

Recommended readings

Ball, S.J. (2016) Neoliberal education? Confronting the slouching beast. *Policy Futures in Education*, 14(8), pp. 1046–1059.
Biesta, G.J.J. (2014) *The Beautiful Risk of Education*. Boulder, CO, and London: Paradigm.
Giddens, A. (1990) *The Consequences of Modernity*. Stanford, CA: Stanford University Press.

References

Arendt, H. (1996) *Sulla Violenza*. Parma: Guanda.
Ball, S.J. (2003) The teacher's soul and the terrors of perfomativity. *Journal of Education Policy*, 18(2), pp. 215–228.
Ball, S.J. (2016) Neoliberal education? Confronting the slouching beast. *Policy Futures in Education*, 14(8), pp. 1046–1059.
Bauman, Z. (2000) *Liquid Modernity*. Cambridge: Polity Press.
Beck, U. (2000) *The Brave New World of Work*. Cambridge: Polity Press.
Benasayag, M. and Schmit, G. (2004) *L'Epoca delle Passioni Tristi*. E. Missana (trans.). Milano: Feltrinelli.
Biesta, G.J.J., Priestley, M. and Robinson, S. (2015) The role of beliefs in teacher agency. *Teachers and Teaching: Theory and Practice*, 21(6), pp. 624–640.
Biesta, G.J.J., Priestley, M. and Robinson, S. (2017) Talking about education: exploring the significance of teachers' talk for teacher agency. *Journal of Curriculum Studies*, 49(1), pp. 38–54.
Bingham, C. (2009) *Authority Is Relational*. Albany, NY: SUNY Press.
Clandinin, D.J. and Connelly, F.M. (1988) *Teachers as Curriculum Planners: Narratives of Experience*. New York: Teachers College Press.
Contreras Domingo, J. (ed.) (2016) *Tensiones Fructíferas. Explorando el saber pedagógico en la formación del profesorado*. Barcelona: Octaedro.
Contreras, D.J. and Pérez De Lara, N. (2010) *Investigar la Experiencia Educativa*. Madrid: Morata.
Cosentino, V. and Santini, M. (eds.) (2008) *L'Amore che non Scordo: Storie di comuni maestre*. Milano: Libreria delle Donne.
Diotima (1995) *Oltre l'Uguaglianza: Le radici femminili dell'autorità*. Napoli: Liguori.
Giddens, A. (1990) *The Consequences of Modernity*. Stanford, CA: Stanford University Press.
Lascioli, A. (2014) *Verso l'Inclusive Education*. Foggia: Edisioni del Rosone 'Franco Marasca'.
Mecenero, M.C. (2004) *Voci Maestre: Esistenze femminili e sapere educativo*. Bergamo: Junior.
Muraro, L. (2013) *Autorità*. Torino: Rosenberg & Sellier.
Nussbaum, M. (2010) *Not for Profit: Why Democracy Needs Humanities*. Princeton, NJ: Princeton University Press.
Pietropolli Charmet, G. (2000) *I Nuovi Adolescenti: Padri e madri di fronte a una sfida*. Milano: Raffaello Cortina Editore.
Pietropolli Charmet, G. (2010) *Fragile e Spavaldo: Ritratto dell'adolescente di oggi*. Roma-Bari: Laterza.
Piussi, A.M. (1990) Towards a pedagogy of sexual difference. *Gender and Education*, 2(1), pp. 81–90.
Piussi, A.M. (2008) *Due Sessi, un Mondo: Educazione e pedagogia alla luce della differenza sessuale*. Verona: Quiedit.
Piussi, A.M. (2011) Il senso libero della libertà: La posta in gioco di una civiltà desiderabile. *Encyclopaideia*, 29(15), pp. 11–46.
Piussi, A.M. (2012) Più del potere, l'autorità. In A. Ascenzi and A. Chionna (eds.), *Potere, Autorità, Formazione: Dinamiche Socio-Culturali*. Bari: Progredit.

5 Illusions of 'choice' in education
Shaping the neoliberal subject in the United Kingdom

Kelly Power

Introduction

Many recent educational policies in the United Kingdom appear to promote 'choice' as a core value, positioning the individual as a 'rational chooser' with the capacity to make informed decisions about their own, or their children's, education. This chapter critically examines this idea, locating it within the economic ideological framework of neoliberalism and suggesting that the rhetoric of 'choice' often serves to conceal strong elements of coercion and central control within the education system. Utilising Foucault's theories of power relations and the processes through which people come to perceive themselves as 'subjects', it explores how neoliberal policy technologies are used to shape and regulate the behaviour of teachers, parents and students. It argues that some 'choices' are highly privileged over others, with a normative vision of the middle-class individual forming the basis for what is seen as good and rational. Additionally, the chapter illustrates the influence of current educational discourses on the self-concepts of working-class children and young people who are often positioned in policy not as rational individuals but as homogeneous products of the school, to be assessed and classified. Education for them is grounded in a neoliberal paternalism that diverges significantly from the philosophical ideals of neoliberal theory.

Defining neoliberalism and its impact on the educated subject

Neoliberalism is a political and economic ideology which values free-market competition and advocates privatisation and reductions in public spending. It differs from classical liberal thought in that it seeks not to reduce the power and scope of the state, but to incorporate the principles of the free market within state operations (Soss *et al.*, 2009). It results in public services being treated as quasi-commodities; their value is quantified and judged by efficiency and return on investment (McGimpsey, 2017). Neoliberalism as an ideology has its origins in Hayekian economic theory of the 1960s, but it rose to prominence in the 1980s as Thatcher's Conservative government transformed the economic and political landscape of Britain, rejecting the Keynesian welfare-state paradigm that had arisen from the post-war consensus. Subsequent governments continued the trend towards neoliberal policies, including the traditionally economically left-wing Labour Party which took power in 1997 under the banner of Blair's 'New Labour' – a neoliberalised government in favour of the 'competition state' (Ball, 2008: 84).

Under neoliberalism, the individual is conceptualised as an autonomous rational actor, capable of achieving success through personal effort and the development of knowledge and skills through education. Structural disadvantages, such as the impact of poverty, are often discursively formulated in neoliberal policy as obstacles or barriers which the successful person has the power to overcome, and not as societal problems in need of a broader solution (see, for instance, Department for Education [DfE], 2017a). To analyse the construction of the neoliberal subject is to examine the processes through which individuals come to perceive and to judge themselves through this neoliberal ideological lens. The 'subject' here is the self-aware individual, possessing a subjective consciousness which has been shaped by the ways in which people are defined and appraised within the narrow confines of ideology. Engagement with the ideas of choice and the rational chooser is one crucial way in which this construction of the subject is enacted in the field of education.

Neoliberal values in educational policy

Before examining the rhetoric of choice in relation to the current educational system, it is perhaps useful to first consider recent trends in government policy and the extent to which educational reforms reflect the core values of neoliberal thought. There is a commitment in policy to developing 'educational excellence' (Gerrard, 2014) which is linked to the ideal of social mobility through participation in a competitive, meritocratic system – that is, one in which success is determined through one's own abilities and efforts, not family wealth or social class. Where large-scale interventions are deemed necessary to address structural disadvantages, they are justified in using the terminology of the market. Notably, a 2011 report recommending additional funding for early years provision was entitled *Early Intervention: Smart Investment, Massive Savings* (Allen, 2011). The rationale for investment was that ensuring educational success in the early years would result in lower state expenditure in the future, as the targeted children would be less likely to suffer a range of negative outcomes, including substance abuse, teenage pregnancy, unemployment, poor health and involvement in crime. Although the report recognised that accurately calculating these 'savings' would be difficult, it suggested that regular assessments for young children, judging their degree of 'school readiness', could be used to measure the effectiveness of the investment (p. xix). This illustrates the market-inspired trend towards quantification of outcomes, however imprecise, in order to justify state funding for new educational initiatives.

Ultimately, the primary purpose of education under neoliberalism is future economic success, both for the individual citizen and for the nation. This is reflected not only in efforts to prevent negative outcomes, but in the focus on 'employability' and skills for work throughout secondary education. Careers guidance given by schools can lead young people to view their studies instrumentally, valuing them only for the future utility of qualifications in the job market. Furthermore, while unpaid 'work experience' placements have not been a statutory requirement in secondary schools since 2012, some schools continue to make them compulsory (Learning and Work Institute, 2017). Often the rhetoric of futurism evident in policy relies on the assumption that participation in formal schooling is the right way, or indeed the only way, to prepare young people to enter the labour market. The Green Paper (Department for Education and Skills [DfES], 2007) which recommended raising the compulsory participation age from 16 to 18 drew on this, implying that those who left at 16 would be unable to develop the skills necessary to succeed at work. Such arguments are predicated upon a particular conceptualisation of 'skills', within the framework of what Ball (2008) describes as the globalised 'knowledge economy' where knowledge and information have replaced capital and energy as the most important factors of production. The only skills worth learning, therefore, are those which serve such an economy. Ball critiques this theory, suggesting not only that it promotes a narrow conceptualisation of education as wholly subordinate to the interests of business, but that the evidence supporting it is 'weak at best' (2008: 23).

The trend towards 'endogenous privatisation' (Ball, 2013: 5) in which schools are treated as businesses, and so become more businesslike, leads not only to an instrumentalist economic view of education within which all state expenditure must be justified on the grounds of outcomes, but also to a complete reshaping of the practices of the school as an institution. One of the most far-reaching of these is the development of a 'performativity' culture under which, because quantified outcomes are used as a proxy for school effectiveness, they are treated as the only educational outcomes that matter. Roberts-Holmes (2015) terms this 'datafication' – a school without 'good data' is deemed to be failing, regardless of the quality of teaching or any wider contextual factors. Neoliberal policy-makers assume that teachers are solely motivated by financial gain or loss (Mortimore, 2013) and so measures to improve data now often include withholding teachers' incremental pay rises unless aspirational targets are met.

It can be seen, then, that the core values of neoliberalism are very much in evidence in recent educational policy initiatives, with a focus on lowering future government expenditure and promoting a particular notion of 'employability' based on the demands of a perceived global 'knowledge economy'. Within schools themselves, performativity measures exemplify an instrumentalist attitude to education whereby expenditure must be justified by improvements in quantified outcomes. What might this approach mean for the children and young people attending these schools? How might it affect their educational experiences?

Questions for reflection

1. Should 'school readiness' be the primary purpose of early years education, and 'employability' the primary purpose of secondary education?
2. What other educational objectives are important? Can (or should) they all be measured?

Foucault, subjectification and the regulatory gaze in education

This section considers the ideological function of schooling and the ways in which schools shape the core values held by children and their internal beliefs. The messages we receive at school, both explicit and implicit, influence our conceptualisations and understandings of ourselves and others. Neoliberal policy technologies in education, therefore, promote a neoliberal worldview in those they act upon. Datafication, for instance, when combined with the increasing lack of trust in teacher professionalism as evidenced by ever-more prescriptive curricular guidance and classroom micro-management by school leaders, creates an overall effect of 'panoptic performativity' (Perryman, 2006) in which teachers feel constantly under surveillance. Perryman characterises the neoliberal school as Foucauldian in its imposition on teachers of a disciplinary regime. Beyond merely altering teachers' behaviour, however, Foucault's theories suggest that the conditions of the school as an institution shape the self-perceptions of those within it, and this is particularly relevant when considering children who are still developing their senses of self and identity.

The notion that the state educational system exists to produce the ideal subject for the state is far from a new one. Marxist theorist Louis Althusser described schools as one of a number of 'ideological state apparatuses' which serve to reproduce the current social order (Althusser, 2006). Along with the overt transmission of knowledge, schools teach an implicit curriculum: societal rules and a degree of respect for the system. Furthermore, he suggested that modern mass-schooling arose in part as a response to declining religiosity among the population. The school replaced the church as a controlling and socialising influence so that the dominant ideology could be normalised and working-class children would grow up fit to meet the needs of the state. Within this framework, educational policy can be used as a 'force of subjectivation' (McGimpsey, 2017: 68) to deliberately shape the self-concepts of individuals. Subjectivation, or subjectification, is the way in which 'human beings are made subjects' (Foucault, 1982: 208) and come to perceive themselves as such; it is intimately interlinked with power relations and systems of domination.

As Foucault said of schools:

> The activity which ensures apprenticeship and the acquisition of aptitudes or types of behaviour is developed there by means of a whole ensemble of regulated communications (lessons, questions and answers, orders, exhortations, coded signs of obedience, differentiation marks of the 'value' of each person and of the levels of knowledge) and by the means of a whole series of power processes (enclosure, surveillance, reward and punishment, the pyramidal hierarchy).
> (1982: 218–219)

These modes of communication and power processes are accepted and internalised by compliant children, and they begin to see themselves as they are seen through the regulatory gaze of the system. Non-compliant children are pathologised, and, under neoliberalism, treated as irrational or incapable and in need of intervention. For Foucault, internal subjectification occurs through processes of objectification, and the process most evident in schools is that of the use of dividing practices. The child is assessed, compared to others and labelled, and these labels – gifted, academic or not, good at maths, sport or art, quiet, disruptive, at-risk, top- or bottom-set – shape that child's identity, not only as a learner but as an individual, and influence their sense of self-worth. The relative value placed on different talents is evident to them, and a performativity culture only intensifies these processes. The primary school child who, having received her test results, and identifies herself as 'I'm a level 3b!' is perhaps an apt illustration.

The rise of performativity culture is one of the most significant effects of neoliberal ideology on the education system. For there to be competition between schools, and to determine which schools provide better returns on the investments the government makes in them, there must be some means by which to compare them. The policy technology of performativity transfers this results-focused outlook from institutions to people, relating 'effort, values, purposes and self-understanding directly to measures and comparisons of output' (Ball, 2013: 12), and placing value only on that which can be quantified. Ball wrote this in reference to the effect that performativity culture has on teachers, but his words are equally applicable to the children that they teach. Teachers are not the only ones acutely aware of their targets. Reflection, self-evaluation and an awareness of the specific ways in which they ought to improve their work to reach the next rung on the assessment ladder are encouraged in even the youngest children. Failing to do so, or actively rejecting the priorities of the institution, is seen as a deviation from the right path, a fault to be rectified.

Choice and competition: education as a free market?

The next section examines the extent to which choice is valued by neoliberal educational policy. Theoretically, the optimal neoliberal system would encourage schools to compete against one another for the custom of parents and students, and would succeed or fail according to market demand. The reality is more complex, and the potential reasons for this will be considered here, using the examples of academies and free schools, qualification reform, and school choice.

Academies and free schools

Another notable aspect of recent policy is that of 'exogenous privatisation' (Ball, 2013: 5) whereby external organisations contribute to the provision of state schooling. Academy schools are funded not by their local education authority (LEA) but directly by the central government. They were originally introduced by the Labour government in 2000 as 'city academies', each with a private sponsor contributing at least £2 million towards school funding. Subsequent policies extended the programme, and after the Academies Act (2010), external sponsors were no longer required and existing schools could become 'converter academies' (Walford, 2014). The city academies were intended to address a specific problem, that of low attainment in urban schools, but later policy developments had the additional focuses of increasing parental choice and school autonomy and reducing the role of the LEAs. The initial converter academies were required to already have an 'outstanding' inspection rating from the Office for Standards in Education (Ofsted), although this was later relaxed (West and Bailey, 2013). Whether the academisation programme as it currently exists is meeting these aims is questionable.

The high value placed on choice was disregarded in favour of a decision to compel all schools to convert to academies, following a policy think-tank report which recommended that all primary schools should become part of academy chains or multi-academy trusts (MATs) by 2020 (Briggs and Simons, 2014). Unpopular with many teachers and local communities, this policy initiative was later abandoned, but by January 2018 almost 7,000 schools had been converted into academies, including 72 per cent of secondary schools. Uptake also varied dramatically between LEAs, with the percentage of academy schools in each ranging from 6 per cent to 93 per cent (DfE, 2018a). Whether autonomy has been increased is a matter of perspective, as academies have more freedom with financial decisions, but teachers often find their autonomy reduced, especially those who have to teach exactly according to the model provided by their MAT (Reay, 2017). The statistics Reay presents also suggest that academisation makes little difference to academic outcomes as judged by Ofsted. Over the period 2012–2016, 73 per cent of academies were assessed as good or outstanding, by comparison to 81 per cent of maintained schools (p. 49).

Free schools are a subset of academies. They are schools proposed by community groups, including parents, teachers, charities and faith groups. The choice of terminology is an intriguing one, with a 'strong anarchist and libertarian history' (Gerrard, 2014: 878). Historically, Gerrard explains, free schools rejected the traditional school system in favour of forms of education which valued working-class or minority cultures, defining educational success in their own terms. However, this radical history is not reflected in contemporary free schools. While any group may apply to open one, Higham (2014) found that the rates of acceptance differed markedly depending on the proposed school ethos and the socioeconomic status of the applicants. Those accepted were predominantly 'professional parents' or mainstream organisations whose educational vision included conservative values and a highly academic curriculum, with a focus on improving standards. Rejected applications, by contrast, tended to be from those with a vocational approach to education, often from disadvantaged urban communities with complex needs. Despite the government's promotion of free schools as autonomous and community-led, these alternative schools are not given the opportunity to even try to compete.

Choice, in this case, is not genuine, but is restricted by an educational conservatism in government which appears to take precedence even over the benefits to future employability that a vocational curriculum might provide. This suggests a conflict between the best interests and perceived economic good of the nation and that of the individual. The highly academic, standards-focused curriculum promotes the skills and values that the neoliberal government considers essential for participation in the 'knowledge economy', and so it chooses to fund schools providing this sort of education. However, the reasoning here is flawed and over-generalised, as the students who are unlikely to succeed within that system cannot choose an alternative, even though a more vocational curriculum would likely lead to greater economic success for them in particular.

The value of qualifications

The devaluation of vocational qualifications is a recurrent characteristic of recent educational reforms. The ambition to raise standards has led to a narrowing of the fields of study that are seen as sufficiently rigorous and academic by which to judge the performance of a school. In 2012, this resulted in the introduction of the English Baccalaureate (EBacc) as a means of measuring success at GCSE level. To achieve the EBacc, a student had to achieve good GCSE passes in English, mathematics, a science subject, a modern foreign language, and either history or geography. It was decried as a 'new philistinism' by Adams (2013) for its complete omission of the creative arts and a failure to recognise their value, not only economically in terms of progression to the creative industries, but also socially. Pring (2013), meanwhile, advanced the argument that if schools are judged on EBacc performance, previously good schools instantly become 'bad', statistically, simply because they have high numbers of students following creative or vocational pathways.

Furthermore, the previous equivalence between GCSEs and vocational qualifications would be lost. Unsurprisingly, many schools adjusted their curricular provision to encourage or require students to take EBacc subjects. A survey investigating its effects found that 27 per cent of schools had withdrawn courses for the 2012/2013 academic year, with drama, art and design technology being the most commonly affected (Greevy et al., 2012). In the schools which made the greatest changes to meet the Ofsted target of 90 per cent of students taking the EBacc, some teachers were critical, with participants in Allen and Thompson's (2016: 5) research study stating that a narrow curriculum was 'not in the best interests' of every student, and that 'results plummeted' leading to 'a high level of disaffection'. It is difficult to see how a limited, prescriptivist curricular model is congruent with an ideology which professes to value both choice and the pursuit of individual educational excellence.

> **Questions for reflection**
>
> 1. Should vocational and creative qualifications have parity with their more academic equivalents?
> 2. Why do you think policy-makers see them as less valuable?

Parental choice narratives

'School choice' is often seen as a cornerstone of the marketisation of education. Instead of being assigned a local school by their LEA, parents would have the freedom to compare schools and choose the one best suited to their child's and family's needs. In practice, the process is less straightforward. Parents list schools in order of preference (between three and six, depending on the area) and places are allocated based on schools' admissions policies, taking these preferences into account. In 2018, 17.9 per cent of applicants did not receive an offer from their first-choice school, and 4.5 per cent were allocated a school which they had not listed as a preference at all. The data varies considerably by area, from Northumberland, where 98.1 per cent were given their first preference, to Hammersmith and Fulham where only 51.4 per cent were (DfE, 2018b). Additionally, the number of feasible options differs not only by location but by socioeconomic status, with the highest quintile having the greatest degree of choice, with better access to 'good' schools (Burgess et al., 2014). For many families, therefore, 'choice' in this matter is entirely illusory. Nonetheless, the narrative of school choice is one which frames the parent as a neoliberal subject, a rational chooser with both the capacity and responsibility to make these critical decisions about their child's education.

Despite these flaws in the system, and the questionable degree to which the implementation of the Academies Act (2010) allows for variety, autonomy and competition, narratives of school choice and the responsibility of the parent as informed chooser not only remain prominent in educational discourse, they also take on moral dimensions. Refusal or inability to engage with the field of choice becomes synonymous with a perceived transgression of parental duties and responsibilities. Under neoliberalism, such duties and responsibilities increasingly take on the character of consumer-oriented dispositions with the economic and affective actor at its centre (Wilkins, 2014: 269–270). Wilkins argues that discourses of school choice simultaneously draw on both rational, economically-oriented patterns of decision-making, and a more emotive, values-focused reasoning, framed in opposition to pure utility. Parents, particularly mothers, are required to navigate skilfully between these two contradictory polarities to choose the right school for their child. As neoliberal subjects, the responsibility for these choices, and their ultimate outcomes, rest with them as individuals, and not the state. If their child is allocated a 'failing' school, the fault is placed with them, for lacking the correct knowledge and dispositions to make a 'better' choice.

However, this is a simplification which ignores both the unequal levels of resources available to parents from different backgrounds, and their relative weighting of different priorities. In a study of school choices, Ball et al. (1996) categorised parents in three broad groups – skilled, semi-skilled and disconnected – and noted a strong correlation between category and social class. What is perhaps most interesting about this study is that the researchers recognise that the 'disconnected' working-class were equally as certain about their choices as the 'skilled' middle-class, but with a very different set of values. Social engagement and local knowledge meant more to them than examination results and other official sources of information. They may have been disconnected from 'choice' in the way policy-makers intended it, but they are not disconnected from their children's welfare and happiness. Choice rhetoric here seems to presuppose that while emotional engagement is essential, it should be subordinated to economically utilitarian rationality, and there is an objectively 'right' choice of school, which aligns with middle-class values.

Finished products? Shaping the neoliberal student

The role of the individual as rational, discerning consumer is not limited to the sphere of education, but a core aspect of neoliberal thought. As previously discussed, the implicit or hidden curriculum functions alongside that which is overtly taught, to shape the inner selves of children in such a way that they perceive the dominant ideology as natural, and thus reproduce it in adulthood. This process is evident from the very beginning of Early Years Foundation Stage (EYFS) education, with curricular documents positioning the successful child as one who makes rational choices during free play, is flexible, and listens to and obeys adult instruction (Bradbury, 2013).

The framing of 'rational choices' is of particular importance to Bradbury who notes in her observations of classroom practice that, while all children are free to choose, not all choices are regarded equally. Those who choose low-status activities, such as physical outdoor play, over high-status ones, like reading and writing, are viewed as less capable. This is perhaps in keeping with the 'school readiness' rhetoric in which failing to meet normative developmental expectations at age five is an indicator that their success, productivity and happiness in adulthood may ultimately be jeopardised. However, it is not compatible with the play-based ethos on which the EYFS curriculum was founded. Even more curious is Bradbury's (2013) finding that children who actively choose all of the activities on offer are seen as better learners than those who concentrate on a select few. This perception appears to owe more to the demands of performativity culture than to developing children's rationality – children must be assessed in every curricular area, and several mention independently-chosen participation as a criterion for achieving the higher standards. The promotion of choice, therefore, is illusory, as the correct, approved choices have been predetermined and are strongly encouraged by practitioners. The indication that a choice is only deemed 'rational' if it is in with keeping with the intent of policy-makers, and with typical middle-class educational values, is not confined to the early years.

The government's 'widening participation' policy initiatives seek to encourage more working-class young people and those from other under-represented minority groups to apply to university, but in doing so, they discursively construct legitimate reasons for non-participation as mere 'barriers' to be overcome (DfE, 2017a, 2017b). Archer *et al.* (2010) reported that their research participants, urban working-class young people, felt that careers advisers placed little value on their wishes to enter employment other than further or higher education, and did not listen to them. Additionally, they were framed as 'at risk' or suffering from 'poverty of aspiration' and thus in need of intervention. Those who leave school early, or refuse to engage, are seen homogeneously as 'less economically viable school "products"' (Maguire, 2012: 249) and a problem to be solved irrespective of the varied reasons for their choices.

Children constructing neoliberal identities

The process of subjectification through schooling results not only in children becoming aware of the relative value they and their choices are assigned within the educational system, it also encourages them to identify with this judgement and to view themselves and others as more or less successful according to neoliberal norms. Whitworth, who examines power and identity-formation through a Foucauldian lens, says this of neoliberalism and the 'entrepreneurial self' which is its ideal subject:

> In terms of its deontology, the aim is not just that entrepreneurial subjects will comply with this vision but more deeply that they will accept and internalise this vision as legitimate and so 'voluntarily' bind themselves to its moral code of individualised risk optimisation.
>
> (2016: 10)

Whitworth's assertion that the development of this outlook is framed in terms of virtue and morality is supported by Morrin's (2018) ethnographic study of an English secondary academy which aims to instil an entrepreneurial mindset in its students. This is defined, not in the more conventional terms of business acumen, but as a 'set of socio-cultural traits and behaviours' (p. 460) which are encouraged in order to develop a certain character. Students earn reward points and badges, described as 'entrepreneurial currency', for displaying certain character traits: determination, passion, creativity, risk-taking, problem-solving and teamwork. Morrin critiques this approach, arguing that it is grounded in a deficit model which assumes that students come to the school possessing none of these positive qualities.

Further, the designation of these broad character traits as 'entrepreneurial' is implicitly ideological. It is possible to possess many of these qualities without adopting the neoliberal 'entrepreneurial mindset', but within the school's scheme they are inseparably interlinked. Students who do not succeed at school are said to lack this correct mindset, and so the problem is perceived as one of weakness of character, ignoring any external factors and absolving the school itself from responsibility. Children and young people who attend schools with values like this often come to believe that they alone are responsible for their academic performance, and that doing well at school, as measured by standardised tests and examinations, is the only way to be assured of a good life. This was evident in one study of high-achieving, mostly middle-class children aged 9–11. These 'children of the market' (Keddie, 2016: 111) had fully internalised the neoliberal discourses of success and performativity. They believed that achievement at school led to economic success, with one participant expressing the thought that without a 'good' job, a person's 'life was over, basically' (p. 112). All were invested in competition against their peers, and maintained that their success was a result of their own efforts and choices. In some cases this led to a lack of empathy, with participants suggesting that those who weren't high achievers simply didn't care enough about their education to try harder. This attitude reveals a certain precariousness inherent in maintaining the identity of the successful young neoliberal subject – many of the children suffered from anxiety, insecurity, self-doubt and maladaptive perfectionism. Believing that your performance at school determines your entire life-course creates a tremendous pressure, and through the process of subjectification, the external pressure from the school system soon becomes internal and self-inflicted.

Control, class and subjectification

The ideal neoliberal subject has been described as 'agentic, individual, choosing, consuming and entrepreneurial' (McGimpsey, 2017: 77), but how far do the material and pedagogical conditions of schools actually cultivate these qualities? The value-structure of a good life being one in which success at school leads to a high-status career is certainly imparted, but for most students, particularly the working class, the everyday practices of the school seem to reinforce character traits in opposition to those overtly promoted. As an institution, the school has much in common with the prison, producing 'docile bodies' (Foucault, 1995) conditioned to obey those in power. The classed nature of this process is made starkly visible through the recent rise of a 'no excuses' ethos in academy schools dedicated to improving attainment: working-class students are tightly controlled, given rules for how to sit and move, where to look, when to speak, and what may be spoken about, in some cases even during their lunch breaks (Graham, 2018). Inflexible and harsh discipline policies lead to sanctions for the smallest mistakes. It seems to be 'as much about punishment as it is about education' (Reay, 2017: 60) and one researcher imagined:

> what it must feel like to be a working-class child in an authoritarian Academy school, where rules are rigid and exceptions are not made, where your culture is disregarded and your home circumstances ignored, where you cannot challenge authority and are often made to feel small, insignificant and powerless.
>
> (Abrahams, 2016, cited in Reay, 2017: 60–61)

It is unlikely that such regimes will produce school-leavers who are agentic individualists capable of making rational choices independently. This treatment appears to owe more to a much older conceptualisation of school as a means to control the working class than to neoliberal ideals. Even in the early years, the aim is to produce, not the educational excellence much vaunted in policy, but dispositions of 'diligence, perseverance, obedience, and participation' (Apple, 2004:53) developed through each child following the same procedures to reach the same outcome for a task. Conventional schools also teach emotional and intellectual dependency (Gatto, 2005) as while students are often encouraged to reflect on their own work, the only opinion that carries weight is that of the teacher. For those who have adopted the values of the school, and who may measure their self-worth by their performance, the teacher is a tremendously powerful figure. Gatto also suggested that schools normalise surveillance as students come to accept that they must be overseen by adults at all times, and are often encouraged to keep watch on each other. The setting of mandatory homework extends that surveillance into the home. In the years since the publication of his work, there has been a rise, particularly in the United Kingdom, of ever-more-intrusive surveillance techniques, including CCTV cameras in schools and biometric scans to monitor attendance at classes and the purchase of lunch, sending detailed reports to parents (Taylor, 2012). These normalise a lack of privacy and condition students to accept government intrusion into, and oversight of, their lives, indicating a degree of authoritarianism at odds with neoliberal philosophy.

> **Questions for discussion**
>
> 1. Consider your own education.
> 2. What values, goals and messages were treated as important, explicitly or otherwise?
> 3. Which did you internalise, and which did you resist?
> 4. How do you think your particular educational experiences have shaped your adult identity, positively or negatively?

Neoliberal paternalism: illusory choice and educational conservatism

It has been argued that while choice is a core value of neoliberalism, and features very prominently in educational policy and rhetoric, the choices made by students, parents and teachers are heavily circumscribed, where they exist at all. Choices that diverge from the middle-class norm are discouraged and often seen as irrational, regardless of the reasons for and circumstances behind them. Such 'irrational' choices are seen as justification for intervention. Therefore, it appears that the educational system as it stands is governed, not by an ideology of pure neoliberalism, but one of neoliberal paternalism, where people, and in particular the working class, are in need of strong oversight and control.

It is important to differentiate this from the idea of 'libertarian paternalism' or 'nudge' politics, also associated with neoliberalism, in which choices are shaped but not restricted. Under this system, the default option is the one that the paternalistic planner prefers, but it is possible to choose otherwise, the logic being that irrational or uninterested individuals are more likely to stay with the default (Mitchell, 2005). Mitchell argues that the term is oxymoronic and runs counter to ideals of liberty, but nonetheless it has made its way into the common lexicon. Neoliberal paternalists, meanwhile, restrict choice as they believe that those affected by their decisions do not have the capacity to make rational choices for themselves. They promote 'a strong state-led effort to bring discipline to the lives of the poor so that they can become competent actors' within the market (Soss et al., 2009: 7).

This attitude is certainly evident in the current treatment of working-class people in education, from community-led free school proposals being turned down to the punitive policies of 'no excuses' academies. Moreover, this paternalistic strand in educational thought is not a new one, but draws on discourses dating back to the advent of universal state education in the late nineteenth century. The rationale behind this was both economic, preparing children to meet the needs of employers in a globally competitive market, and moral, attempting to guide working-class children towards middle-class norms in values and conduct. The description in policy of educators as 'agents of improvement' in promoting social mobility (DfE, 2017a), with its reliance on a discourse of deficit, would not have been out of place in a nineteenth-century text. Through the school system, children are made subjects, and the subject-position of the working-class child is often that of the 'Other', for whom success, defined in narrow instrumentalist terms, is only possible if the norms and values of the institution are accepted and internalised, and the 'right' choices made.

Conclusion

While the rhetoric of choice is evident in much of neoliberal educational policy, the choices available to individuals are often limited and restricted by those in power. A school with a conservative curriculum and ethos is far more likely to gain the approval of the authorities than one with a more innovative or community-centred outlook, and a performativity culture discourages schools from promoting vocational or creative pathways to students. Through systems of regulation, control and classification, individuals undergo a process of subjectification in which their identity is shaped by the value-judgements that they internalise. For the child living under neoliberalism, this is likely to include the idea that their performance at school, good or bad, is entirely within their control and will determine their future success. Neoliberal ideology values individualistic, rational and entrepreneurial citizens. Yet these qualities are unlikely to be developed by a system which treats students as the interchangeable products by which competing schools are judged, assuming that all should learn in the same way and at the same pace. Instead, it is argued, working-class students are socialised towards a narrow conformity, intellectual dependence, and the acceptance of the judgements of authority.

Education for many working-class families, therefore, is grounded not in pure neoliberal ideology, but a distinct 'neoliberal paternalism' which seeks to control and direct while maintaining the illusion of free choice. This serves to entrench division between working- and middle-class families, while maintaining that meritocratic social mobility is possible for all – but only if middle-class ideals are adopted. Those who fail to do this, or actively resist it, are deemed irrational and in need of greater paternalistic control. What would a purely neoliberal education system look like? Along with the privatisation would come a much greater variety in school choice, with vocational qualifications which led to specific fields of employment being highly valued. Students would be encouraged to discover their own particular talents, and develop them with a view to future employability. Schools would encourage genuine choice and agency from an early age as well as promoting entrepreneurial values, in order to develop the power of rational decision-making in students from all backgrounds. It would be recognised that an optimal decision about qualifications, further or higher education might look very different for one person than another, depending on their values, abilities and circumstances, and so there would be no coercion or condemnation of 'wrong' choices. While it is not a vision of education that everyone would approve of, it would be radically, and thought-provokingly, different from the paternalistic one of the present.

Summary points

- Neoliberalism seeks to incorporate the principles of the free market into state services. This has led to schools being run more like businesses, including a strong focus on outcomes and value for investment resulting in a performativity culture.
- Subjectification is the way in which people come to perceive themselves as subjects. This occurs through power relations and systems of classification which shape an individual's identity and sense of self.
- Choice is seen as an important part of neoliberal education policy, but in practice certain choices are considered legitimate and valuable, while others are restricted or discouraged. These distinctions are heavily classed in nature.
- Many pedagogical practices in schools are designed not to foster individualism, independence and agency, which are qualities of the ideal neoliberal subject, but docility, dependency and obedience.
- Educational policies are grounded, not in pure neoliberalism, but in a neoliberal paternalism which does not recognise the capacity of working-class people to make rational decisions according to their own interests, but seeks to control them.

Recommended readings

Ball, S. (2008) *The Education Debate* (2nd edition). Bristol: Policy Press.
Foucault, M. (1982) The subject and power. In H. Dreyfus and P. Rabinow (eds.), *Michel Foucault: Beyond Structuralism and Hermeneutics*. Brighton: Harvester Press.
Reay, D. (2017) *Miseducation: Inequality, Education and the Working Classes*. Bristol: Polity Press.

References

Academies Act (2010) (c. 32). London: HMSO.
Adams, J. (2013) The English baccalaureate: a new philistinism? *International Journal of Art & Design Education*, 32(1), pp. 2–5.
Allen, G. (2011) *Early Intervention: Smart Investment, Massive Savings*. London: HMSO.
Allen, R. and Thompson, D. (2016) *Changing the Subject: How Are the EBacc and Attainment 8 Reforms Changing Results?* Research Brief Edition 13. London: Sutton Trust.
Althusser, L. (2006) *Lenin and Philosophy and Other Essays*. Delhi: Aakar Books.
Apple, M. (2004) *Ideology and Curriculum* (3rd edition). London: RoutledgeFalmer.
Archer, L., Hollingworth, S. and Mendick, H. (2010) *Urban Youth and Schooling*. Maidenhead: McGraw-Hill/Open University Press.
Ball, S. (2008) *The Education Debate* (2nd edition). Bristol: Policy Press.
Ball, S. (2013) *Neoliberal Education? Confronting the Slouching Beast*. Vere Foster Public Lecture, National Gallery of Ireland, Dublin, 26 February.
Ball, S., Bowe, R. and Gewirtz, S. (1996) School choice, social class and distinction: the realization of social advantage in education. *Journal of Education Policy*, 11(1), pp. 89–112.
Bradbury, A. (2013) Education policy and the 'ideal learner': producing recognisable learner-subjects through early years assessment. *British Journal of Sociology of Education*, 34(1), pp. 1–19.
Briggs, A. and Simons, J. (2014) *Primary Focus: The Next Stage of Improvement for Primary Schools in England*. London: Policy Exchange.
Burgess, S., Greaves, E., Vignoles, A. and Wilson, D. (2014) What parents want: school preferences and school choice. *Economic Journal*, 125, pp. 1262–1289.
Department for Education (2017a) *Unlocking Talent, Fulfilling Potential (Cm 9541)*. London: HMSO.
Department for Education (2017b) *Understanding the Changing Gaps in Higher Education Participation in Different Regions of England: Research Report*. London: HMSO.
Department for Education (2018a) *Converting Maintained Schools to Academies (HC 720)*. London: National Audit Office.
Department for Education (2018b) *Secondary and Primary School Applications and Offers: March and April 2018*. London: HMSO.
Department for Education and Skills (2007) *Raising Expectations: Staying in Education and Training Post-16*. Norwich: HMSO.
Foucault, M. (1982) The subject and power. In H. Dreyfus and P. Rabinow (eds.), *Michel Foucault: Beyond Structuralism and Hermeneutics*. Brighton: Harvester Press.
Foucault, M. (1995) *Discipline and Punish: The Birth of the Prison* (2nd edition). A. Sheridan (trans.). New York: Vintage Books.
Gatto, J. (2005) *Dumbing Us Down: The Hidden Curriculum of Compulsory Schooling*. Gabriola Island, Canada: New Society Publishers.
Gerrard, J. (2014) Counter-narratives of educational excellence: free schools, success, and community-based schooling. *British Journal of Sociology of Education*, 35(6), pp. 876–894.
Graham, L. (2018) Student compliance will not mean 'all teachers can teach': a critical analysis of the rationale for 'no excuses' discipline. *International Journal of Inclusive Education*, 22(11), pp. 1242–1256.
Greevy, H., Knox, A., Nunney, F. and Pye, J. (2012) *The Effects of the English Baccalaureate: Research Report DFE-RR249*. London: DfE.
Higham, R. (2014) Free schools in the big society: the motivations, aims and demography of free school proposers. *Journal of Education Policy*, 29(1), pp. 122–139.
Keddie, A. (2016) Children of the market: Performativity, neoliberal responsibilisation and the construction of student identities. *Oxford Journal of Education*, 42(1), pp. 108–122.
Learning and Work Institute (2017) *Work Experience Programmes: Briefing Paper for the Department of Education, June 2017*. Leicester: National Learning and Work Institute.
Maguire, M. (2012) Identity work in a London primary school: a head teacher's perspective. In W. Pink (ed.), *Schools for Marginalized Youth: An International Perspective*. New York: Hampton Press.
McGimpsey, I. (2017) Late neoliberalism: delineating a policy regime. *Critical Social Policy*, 37(1), pp. 64–84.
Mitchell, G. (2005) Libertarian paternalism is an oxymoron. *Northwestern University Law Review*, 99(3), pp. 1245–1277.
Morrin, K. (2018) Tensions in teaching character: how the 'entrepreneurial character' is reproduced, 'refused', and negotiated in an English academy school. *Sociological Research Online*, 23(2), pp. 459–476.

Mortimore, P. (2013) *Education under Siege*. Bristol: Policy Press.
Perryman, J. (2006) Panoptic performativity and school inspection regimes: disciplinary mechanisms and life under special measures. *Journal of Education Policy*, 21(2), pp. 147–161.
Pring, R. (2013) Another reform of qualifications – but qualifying for what? *Political Quarterly*, 84(1), pp. 139–143.
Reay, D. (2017) *Miseducation: Inequality, Education and the Working Classes*. Bristol: Polity Press.
Roberts-Holmes, G. (2015) The 'datafication' of early years pedagogy: 'If the teaching is good, the data should be good and if there's bad teaching, there is bad data'. *Journal of Education Policy*, 30(3), pp. 302–315.
Soss, J., Fording, R. and Schram, S. (2009) Governing the Poor: The Rise of the Neoliberal Paternalist State. Paper presented at the Annual Meeting of the American Political Science Association, Toronto.
Taylor, E. (2012) The rise of the surveillance school. In K. Ball, K. Haggerty and D. Lyon (eds.), *Routledge Handbook of Surveillance Studies*. London: Routledge.
Walford, G. (2014) Academies, free schools and social justice. *Research Papers in Education*, 29(3), pp. 263–267.
West, A. and Bailey, E. (2013) The development of the academies programme: 'Privatising' school-based education in England 1986–2013. *British Journal of Education Studies*, 61(2), pp. 137–159.
Whitworth, A. (2016) Neoliberal paternalism and paradoxical subjects: confusion and contradiction in UK activation policy. *Critical Social Policy*, 36(3), pp. 412–431.
Wilkins, A. (2014) Affective labour and neoliberal fantasies: the gendered and moral economy of school choice in England. In M. Vandenbeld Giles (ed.), *Mothering in the Age of Neoliberalism*. Ontario: Demeter Press.

6 An exploration of human capital theory and its effects on the world of education

Halil Buyruk

Introduction

Human Capital Theory (HCT) plays an important part in the effects the economy has on education and in describing the economic role of education. According to HCT, individuals acquire knowledge and skills called human capital through a number of activities, mainly through education and training. The knowledge and skills acquired raise humans' productive capacity. It is claimed that the increase in production capacity and in labour productivity leads to economic growth and that individuals get more shares from the increase in welfare. Another point that HCT stresses is that humans' expenditures on activities such as education and training to increase their productivity can be considered as an investment. Individuals invest in themselves through education which will turn them into a qualified workforce to raise their income in the future and that they become capital for themselves. This line of reasoning basically indicates two changes. The first is that the rational individuals who consider education only as an instrument to increase their capital search for an education through which they can make a good investment. The second is that the educational processes are transformed on the axis of economy, in a manner so as to raise a qualified workforce as associated with the first one. In accordance with the theory, the goals and content of education – described as an economic variable – are set through time on the axis of improving workforce efficiency, increasing productivity and thus contributing to economic growth. While this rationality causes education to be shaped to meet the needs of the economy, it also leads us to ignore the cultural and social dimensions of education, and the possibility of an education which is not tightly linked to economic outcomes.

The meaning of education is filled with more economic content today, and efforts are made to configure the educational system consistently with neoliberal models. Discussions on education are more influenced by using economic concepts; the field of education becomes re-interpretable through these concepts and is regulated consistently within economic rationality. Schools are designed to raise productive workers along with these developments which we can describe as the economisation of education, and curricula from pre-school to HE are re-shaped according to an entrepreneurial model in which the individual needs to strive to forge a successful future in a competitive environment. Such concepts as 'cost/benefit', 'investment', 'competition' and 'customer' are frequently used in the description of education and in the functioning of educational processes. Global organisations such as Organisation for European Economic Co-operation and Development (OECD) and the World Bank play significant roles in the global spread of such an educational model because they play active parts in configuring education around HCT with the loans they provide, the policies they implement and thus the economisation of education.

This chapter firstly describes the historical development of HCT in general terms and looks at some criticisms concerning the theory. It then focuses on the role HCT plays in the economisation of education. The final section explains the contemporary role of HCT and its effects on educational policies along with the roles of global actors.

HCT: the historical context

Several economists have pointed out that education and training create value in the form of knowledge and skills and thus increase the production capacity of the human force, just as investment in a machine increases the production capacity of physical capital stock (Woodhall, 1987). For example, Adam Smith (1776/1976), the author of *The Wealth of Nations*, claimed that an educated man could be compared to expensive machines, and stated that investment in education could be regarded as a form of investment which would be beneficial in the future. Marshall (1890/2013), who thought that the most valuable of all capital investments was the one made in humans, was interested in developments in human quality and considered quality-increasing activities such as education as capital investment. Many of the classical economists such as Smith and Marshall drew attention to the importance of education and created the premise that the investment made would be paid back through increased productivity.

The origins of modern HCT are based on the works of Schultz (1960, 1961) and Becker (1964), who were connected with the Chicago School which played an important role in the development of neoliberal economic thinking. Humans were for the first time made the subject of economic analysis as an economic category with the label 'human capital' in the works of these economists. Beginning with this period, studies have focused on such issues as the contribution of education to economic growth, the role of an educated human force in economic development and the profitability of educational investments, the economic value of education, the cost and financing of education (Woodhall, 1987).

Although HCT spans ideas such as measuring human capital, human capital and economic growth, human capital and income distribution, human capital investment, it centres mainly on two themes. One of the themes is the relations wage differences and/or income distribution have/has with education and training. One of the first studies conducted in this area is *Investment in Human Capital and Personal Income Distribution* by Mincer (1958). The author considers the relations between personal income distribution and investment in human capital and concludes that education and training affect personal income distribution. Another study by Schultz (1960) – referring to human force as 'capital' – describes time, source, training, etc. allocated to education as investment which will later yield high profit in the form of people who can pay back their way into society by working and paying taxes. Thus, education and training which had been considered only as consumption before were from that time on considered as investment.

Another remarkable tendency in studies concerning HCT is the fact that investment in human capital increases productivity and therefore results in economic growth. This approach is based on the claim that the quality of workforce can be improved through education and training. In contrast to the classical view of ignoring differences in the quality of workforce, HCT calls attention to the qualitative aspects of workforce, and workforce is described as 'heterogeneous'. Denison (1962), one of pioneers who studied the contributions of education to economic growth, tried to determine the contributions of different factors of production to the national income increase in the United States. Denison claimed that the development in the quality of workforce was important to growth and claimed that the parts unexplained in growth calculations could stem from education – that is to say, increase in human capital. According to Denison, increase in the educational level of workforce in the period between 1930 and 1960 explains a considerable part – 23 per cent – of the annual rate of growth of the gross national product (GNP) in the United States. Schultz (1961), suggesting that economic growth cannot be analysed without using the concept of human capital, contends that education makes direct contributions to the growth of national income by raising the production capacity and skills of the workforce.

Becker (1993), having an important role in the development of HCT, focuses in his book *Human Capital* on activities which will influence financial and psychological income in the future through the development of human resources. Becker, stating that education is the most important investment in human capital, considers on-the-job-training, medical care, migration and searching for information about prices and incomes are forms of investment in human capital. All of these investments, which are different in their effects on income and consumption, in investment costs, in returns and in perception improve skills, knowledge and health increase financial and psychological income (Becker, 1993).

The basic arguments suggested by HCT were developed throughout the 1960s. Activities of any type increasing humans' production capacity – mainly education and training – came under the heading of human capital and were described as investment. It was claimed that increase in human capital stock was caused by education and training increases the amount of production. Investment in humans brings about a rise in productivity; it raises wages on the one hand and contributes to economic growth on the other. Therefore, economy and human capital are interrelated in two ways.

> **Question for reflection**
>
> 1. What are the main arguments of the HCT developed in the 1960s?

Criticisms of HCT

Several criticisms directed to HCT are available. Some alternative approaches call attention to missing elements of the theory, whereas others criticise HCT more radically. The approaches calling attention to the inadequacies of the theory consider education from an economic perspective, just as HCT does, and they describe the role of education in the economy as an 'alternative approach'. One of those criticisms of HCT comes from the Screening Hypothesis (Arrow 1973; Spence 1973). According to this hypothesis, education functions as a mechanism classifying individuals according to their abilities, achievement and motivation and labelling them with various documents (Blaug, 1976). Educational gains are descriptive of abilities of certain types and levels in the market. Thus, individuals at differing levels of productivity are described, labelled and eliminated through education (Unal, 1996). According to this hypothesis, education does not directly affect efficiency, it only provides employers with information on applicants' abilities. Thus, it is argued in the Screening

Hypothesis that there are indirect rather than direct relations between education and efficiency. For example, having an elite university degree gives a signal to employers about the abilities of individuals who are in line for the job. According to this signal, the employers know whether applicants have the abilities they expect when making decisions on recruitment. This assumption has brought criticism of the Screening Hypothesis, arguing that there are other means selecting employees, and that education is an expensive mechanism simply for describing capabilities (Kjelland, 2008).

Another criticism of HCT comes from the Theory of Segmented Labour Markets (Cain, 1976). This theory points to the differences in the labour market, not in systems of education, as one of the most important variables determining work conditions and wages. The market is not considered as a whole and is seen as segments having different functionings and is analysed in this way. Technological circumstances, payment structures, rise conditions and human capital investment returns are different for each segment of the market (Unal, 1996). Market segments are usually analysed in a dual structure as primary and secondary markets. Primary markets involve jobs in which big companies, unions, job security and career opportunities are available, and wages are relatively high (Blaug, 1985). Secondary markets involve jobs in which work conditions are bad, there are no unions and involve mostly small companies. Since more labour supply is available in secondary markets in general, where there is high competition, wages are low. Jobs in such markets are insecure. A HCT approach would purport that these individuals face these challenges because of their lack of education and that the solution to the problem is to improve educational opportunities and outcomes. According to the Theory of Segmented Labour Markets, however, increase in the duration of education does not turn into gains and is not influential in decreasing poverty, nor can it assure social justice since human capital needs diverse and fair employment markets for people to see the rewards of education. Think about how there have been problems in recent years with the high numbers of graduates who are going into employment markets affected by the recent credit crises and who have to take worse paid jobs, not because they don't have the skills, but because the jobs the markets offer have worse employment conditions and lower pay.

Another basic criticism of HCT is that it does not recognise the distinction between labour and labour-power. Since HCT does not make such a distinction, humans are described as a commodity. However, the commodity is the labour-power described with a physical and mental capacity, skills and behavioural characteristics of the individual contributing to the production process (Marx, 2011). In addition, HCT has the tendency to blur the distinction between labour and capital, and thus to state that a worker possesses capital (Bowles and Gintis, 1975). Such an approach describes labour inside capital and doesn't consider social class as a central concept. Thus, HCT, whose focal point is not the concept of class, isolates class conflicts. However, it is argued that the phenomena such as educational process and wage structure can only be interpreted through class analysis (Bowles and Gintis, 1975). Therefore, HCT isolates the social relations available in production and considers them as a technical relation.

The approach of the HCT to the access to education and the choice of profession are also subject to criticism. According to Marxist approaches, individuals' demands for education and their choice of profession are not the result of their individual, free and rational decisions as argued in HCT, but are determined by their class position. Educational systems distribute individuals coming from different social classes according to the types and levels of education fitting their social class, and instruct them into accepting their position without the possibility of contestation (Althusser,

2006). Skills individuals gain through education differ according to schools of differing types and levels preparing staff for differing jobs. For instance, while behavioural properties such as punctuality, amenableness, adaptiveness and ability to work with others are gained in schools training individuals for lower level jobs personal traits such as self-respect, self-confidence, versatility and leadership capacity are reinforced in universities preparing individuals for higher-level professions (Bowles and Gintis, 1976). At the end of the process, children are usually distributed to jobs similar to those of their parents. However, education does not sign individuals according to their natural abilities as claimed in the Screening Hypothesis while performing this distribution function. On the contrary, it eliminates them according to their skills developed by social factors, and ensures that they are distributed to various jobs with qualifications offered. Therefore, contrary to what is claimed in HCT, it cannot be said that education plays an effective role in determining the occupational positions and the formation of wage differences as much as social factors.

Neoliberalism, HCT and the economisation of education

After Foucault, Brown (2015) defines neoliberalism as management rationality, ensuring the process of economisation containing all the dimensions of human life. Economisation refers to the transformation of living areas which were not described in terms of economy according to market rules and in accordance with economic rationality. Social relations are transformed in accordance with the requirements of economy. In this neoliberal framework, economic rationality functioning in the transformation of public and political spheres and of subjects and practices in accordance with the models of market is expanded into non-economic areas. Thus, this new rationality spreads into every field from law to education, and economises the areas it spreads into and re-shapes the human spirit as *homo economicus* (Brown, 2015).

The basic assumptions of the neoclassic economic model about human behaviours should be outlined to get a clear and complete picture of HCT (Tan, 2014). The neoclassic model considers individuals as the decision-making units in an atomistic approach. The model assumes that individuals who display rational behaviours try to maximise their economic benefits. Individuals who make a choice between several options will choose the option which provides them the maximum benefit, or which will bring them the highest profit. Thus, an individual who behaves rationally is always assumed to do economic analyses as a *homo economicus*. Yet, the *homo economicus* of the recent neoliberal period has differences in some respects, even though it is similar to the *homo economicus* of the classical economic thought. *Homo economicus* as an economic person, a person who struggles in accordance with his needs in its classical sense. In the neoliberal period, however, *homo economicus* is an entrepreneur, a company, a company of his own and his own capital (Foucault, 2008). That is, he doesn't just do economic analysis or strive for economic benefit. He is now a capital owner who constantly invests in himself and increases his capital. The aim of the individual who invests in himself as a market actor is not merely the accumulation of economic wealth. The individual is an entrepreneur with economic reasoning. Such an entrepreneurial individual can provide non-economic areas to be reinterpreted with purely economic terms and thus to be economised (Foucault, 2008).

HCT has impacted and shaped what we think about and how we interpret education. Arguments made to see and treat education as an important part of economics can be understood with ideas of what the term 'education' means. Education is derived from two Latin words which are similar in spelling and in pronunciation (Billington, 2003). One of those words is 'educare' which meant 'making someone drill', 'moulding' which helps learners to acquire a number of skills so that they can attain different goals which may be connected with getting a job. The goal of this education is shaped in the context of raising individuals as labour-power equipped with qualifications required by the economy, as good citizens, compatible with current social structure and as consumers who have internalised market values (Özsoy, 2002). The content of such education is based on an instrumental and pragmatic approach and focuses on outcome rather than process in relation to its purpose. The other word is 'educere' which meant 'lead out'. Education shaped on the basis of this principle is a process enabling individuals to explore the world and individuals themselves without any utilitarian reason and to become authorised by, which helps them to become autonomous. The goal of this education, as different from disciplining, is to uncover individuals' capacity to take on their own responsibility – that is to say, to uncover their capacity to make themselves the subject of their relations with themselves, with others and with the world (Gorz, 2001). Ideas and skills to be gained in such a process of education are pursued not only for external reasons such as the purpose they will serve but also because they and the acquisition process are valuable – that is to say, for internal reasons. Only in this way can individuals comprehend their potential, discover their abilities and develop in multiple ways. Contrary to education shaped in the framework of raising 'efficient workers' in the approach of 'educare', the questions of what to do and what goals to attain with knowledge and skills gained through education in the meaning of 'educere' become meaningless. This is because education is not seen as instrumental and the process itself becomes valuable. We can say that the two meanings of education can exist together despite their contrast, but that the current hegemony relations shape the goals, content and practices of education. In this framework, we can express education shaped according to HCT as the hegemony and prevalence of education in the meaning of 'educare', and thus as the marginalisation of education in the meaning of 'educere'. While analysing education in terms of economy and representing it in economic terms, HCT-based applications cause it to become instrumental and to be shaped according to the needs of economy. It ensures that education in the sense of educare becomes widespread. Thus, HCT not only makes education the subject of economic analysis, but also economises education and re-builds education in the framework of economic reasoning.

HCT also determines the way individuals who are to receive education should behave. According to the basic argument of HCT, individuals make calculations of benefit-cost. It is assumed in this context that parents also do benefit-cost analysis in choosing a school for their children by calculating their expenditures and what they get in return. According to HCT, employees having higher human capital accumulation, have higher productivity and are paid higher wages. Rational individuals who are knowledgeable about these calculations and observing the labour market evaluate the returns their education will offer them and the cost they will have to encounter throughout their education. Employment opportunities and expectations for wage after graduation are especially important in the process of evaluation. Another factor influential in decisions to invest further in education is the cost of education and opportunity. Individuals will invest in education if they believe that the returns will be more than the cost according to their benefit-cost calculations. This naturally means that educational decisions are isolated from desire for pleasure or that such goals are considered in a manner quantitatively comparable with goals of earning by taking into consideration the opportunities to earn (Bugra, 1995). For instance, an individual's decision to study Japanese occurs as a result of his calculation of the benefits this activity will offer him. If the individual finds that the benefits of studying Japanese will be bigger than the cost of it, he begins to study Japanese. Education is interpreted through the needs of the economy. The cultural and social values of education become ignored if all the benefits of education are expressed in economic terms. Education is shaped more and more on the basis of providing individuals with occupation or with skills to secure economic growth in a utilitarian approach (Spring, 2015). One of the reflections of this into educational institutions is the removal from the curriculum of subjects and courses which are not skill-based or attaching less importance to such courses. Education is basically thought to be an economic activity and the knowledge and skills learnt at school are thought to be the capital for use in economic activities. In this framework, curriculum is re-shaped from pre-school to HE on the basis of entrepreneurial education.

HCT is important in that it demonstrates how a subject is fictionalised on the basis of rationality for itself as capital in the neoliberal period. While this fiction explains that individuals make choices in the area of education with their economic reason, it also plays active roles in the transformation of other actors related to education, because the question about for what probable purpose and motive all actors in education will use their capital is determined in this framework of rationality. Educational processes that people who invest in themselves on the axis of economic rationality are also the outcomes of similar rationality. Such rationality changes the whole field of education from making educational decisions at national and even global levels to school management, from employment and evaluation of educational staff to creating the curriculum, from school choice to measurement and evaluation system. Hence, a performance evaluation system is used today in teacher evaluation as in many companies, and an environment of competition in which they will be more productive is created. In a similar vein, while the standardised examinations students have to take at different levels lead to a competition-based functioning on the one hand, they can also be used in measuring school performance on the other. Thus, decisions about education are made rationally in consequence of economic analysis and practices are shaped accordingly.

Questions for reflection

1. How have ideas about the cost-benefit analysis affected ideas of education?
2. What does it mean if learning is understood as an economic activity?

Global actors, educational policies and timeliness of HCT

The OECD has an important role in implementing HCT in various areas of the world. It has played an active role in the increase in public investment in education, especially with the relations it set up between education and economic development. Yet neoliberal policies which began to dominate in the 1980s made it obligatory to update the educational policies of the OECD. This was because the role of the state increased in favour of the market, while the function of the state shrank in funding social services in this new period when the state itself was being transformed, and approaches which might be the basis for educational investment needed to be revised. Therefore, while efforts were made to increase the share of private investment in education on the one hand, skill-providing policies were included on the other. In recent years, the OECD has implemented policies of providing job-related skills and has stressed that the skills to be provided should not be restricted to schools (OECD, 2014). The OECD, acting for the globalisation of educational policies it has formed, has globalised educational knowledge about countries in different regions of the world through the educational indicators it broadcasts. Human capital accumulation in various countries has been measured by the OECD in recent years through various tests, and a comparison of human capital accumulation has been made between countries. Those tests which are determinant in measuring and developing the qualities necessary for the economy, and which are given on international scale, are one of the areas where global competition between states is seen. States set out from the assumption that knowledge obtained through those tests inform us of the future economy of countries, and thus states can see their opponents' ranking by means of performance-based league tables. Yet, those tests do not take knowledge and pedagogy differences into consideration and reduce them into technical problems in comparing student achievement globally (Lauder et al., 2012).

Another organisation playing roles in the global influence of HCT-based policies is the World Bank. The organisation was influential in setting up the relations between education and economy by focussing on the development of third-world countries, even though it was not directly interested in this issue in the years when it was founded. The bank gives credit and technical support to developing countries so as to support educational projects, to reduce poverty and to help those countries develop. It offers training throughout the globe and ensures that an economic approach is adopted and spreads the educational policies it wishes to implement. For instance, the World Bank contributes significantly to human capital education through e-learning courses in the field of educational economy, describing the goal of those courses as helping educational leaders in making decisions about educational reforms by using such economic instruments as HCT, rate of return and individual and social benefits (Spring, 2015). In this way, educators will be able to think like an economist at the end of the course, spread these ideas further and support future policies and policy-making.

The World Bank plays important roles in shaping educational policies in the international arena with the donations and loans it gives, and it makes its policies widespread in many countries through the programmes and projects it supports. The World Bank first shaped educational policies suitable to Keynesian policies on the axis of planning raising human force necessary for the development of states. It began to change those policies in the period after 1980 so as to instigate the labour qualifications required by markets. It took an active role in the adoption of widespread neoliberal policies in this process. It played a significant role in localising education, renewing curricula and in privatising schools through conditional loans. It may be said that the educational policies of World Bank follow HCT policies. Even though differing tendencies can be mentioned, the focal point is to raise qualified human force for economic development (see World Bank, 2005). It provides support and loans for the projects it supports so as to be able to make investment in line with the purpose. For example, Turkey has completed seven World Bank–funded projects in the field of education since 1985 (MoNE, 2019). One of the largest is the Basic Education Project; another is the National Education Development Project. These projects have played important roles in developing new educational managerialism, flexibility in teacher employment and increasing the sensitivity of education to the labour market. Having roles in shaping global educational policies, the World Bank emphasises the knowledge and skills which are instigated through education in the conceptualisation of the knowledge economy and thus ensures that the lifelong learning approach remains on the agenda.

> **Question for reflection**
>
> 1. What parts do international organisations have in configuring educational systems on the basis of HCT?

The timeliness of HCT

The conceptualisation of the 'knowledge society' or 'knowledge economy' emphasises the importance of knowledge in social structures and in that the economy has increased in parallel to developments in information and communication technologies. The knowledge-based economy concept – which is based on the argument that the importance of knowledge has been increasing in the process of production – points to the need that economies and societies should be built on the basis of knowledge in order for them to be sustainable. A knowledge-economy approach, which may be seen as different from HCT, is fundamentally based on renewed HCT. This contemporary form of HCT has been extended to preserve the superiority of individuals, companies and governments in line with the requirements of the global economy in the previous form of the theory (Rizvi and Lingard, 2010). Even though the new theory is claimed to have different dimensions, it is basically built on the foundation of individuals acting for their economic benefits in a free market under competitive circumstances. In this approach, which is based on the definition of rational individuals, it is claimed that performance is more dependent on humans' accumulation of knowledge, their levels of skills, learning capacity and cultural adjustment in a global economy. Therefore, importance is attached to policies of increasing labour flexibility required by the new economy and it is stressed that reforms are needed in the educational system to meet all these requirements. In this framework, policies for re-arranging educational systems and for re-defining the goals of education are accelerated. Uzunyayla and Ercan (2009) state that educational policies were shaped on the aim of raising a workforce that would be competitive, would adapt to technological changes rapidly, would generate and apply technological knowledge and would learn to learn so as to be able to adjust to rapid changes in accordance with employment policies in the last quarter of the twentieth century. Therefore, lifelong learning is considered to be a way of providing workforce qualifications which are changing and of employees' renewal of themselves according to a changing labour market, and emphasis is laid on the continuity of this process. This is because the shelf life of skills is getting shorter in the modern economy. As in technology, science or advanced forms of production, workers should be trained again every eight or ten years (Sennett, 2006). The lifelong learning approach suggests that human capital, which is worn out through time, should continuously be renewed. Contemporary HCT may be said to differ from the traditional one in this respect. Traditional HCT assumed that investment in humans would lead to an increase in labour productivity and in wages. According to contemporary HCT, however, this investment should continuously be renewed so as to meet the skills required by economy. Therefore, while the process of formal education is shaped by reforms to provide new workforce qualifications, the lifelong learning approach recommends that this process should never end: the workforce should immediately adapt to the changing production organisation, to technology and to the new conditions in order not to be made redundant.

An exploration of human capital theory   73

Investing in education is defined as a necessity in order to achieve a high-income job in a knowledge economy where education and learning mean to gain high income and status. The content of learning is largely shaped according to the labour-force qualities that companies need. While subjective and cultural differences are not taken into account during educational processes, the focus is on the education which contributes to productivity. This new educational approach, which requires the individual to select and get the most appropriate one for his/her needs, transforms the knowledge and skills into a kind of education package that can be bought and sold. Thus, the field of education, which is not limited to school, creates a new market with the skills-based certificate programmes it provides. It is an individual choice for a rational person to invest in such an education for lifelong gains, as claimed in HCT. Yet, the objective is to globalise the qualifications which are intended to be developed today; and this necessitates investment in education. However, employers needing a qualified workforce avoid making major investment in education, and to a large extent, governments take on this duty. But individuals investing in education, as stated in HCT, obtain benefits to a large extent. For this reason, the cost is paid by individuals in recent years due to the principle formulated as 'the one who benefits will pay'. While the schooling process is less focused on in the age of the knowledge economy than in traditional HCT, an approach considering learning properties that individuals can develop is seen as important in being able to cope with changing work conditions and aiming to develop human resources. This meant individuals providing the qualifications needed, on the one hand, and it opened doors to the policies of privatising education, on the other.

Conclusion

Many economists have pointed out that education and training create value in the form of knowledge and skills and thus increase production capacity, and that expenditures in education can be regarded as a form of investment which may provide benefits in the future (Woodhall, 1987). This approach, which was called HCT in the 1960s, basically focuses on the economic role of education and puts activities of any type increasing humans' production capacity under the title of human capital and describes them as an investment. It is claimed accordingly that this investment can be used in describing individual income differences and leads to economic growth by promoting labour productivity. However, the theses argued by HCT have received criticism over time. It is claimed that direct relationship cannot be set up between education and efficiency and that various factors – mainly the differences in labour market – can be influential in explaining the income differences. Another criticism of HCT is that the theory isolates the social relations in production and that it considers the relations as technical relations. Despite the criticisms, HCT plays active roles in the economisation of education in the neoliberal period and in its transformation on the basis of economic priorities.

Neoclassical arguments, on which HCT is based, regard individuals as having economic rationality and the design of a society composed of a sum of such individuals. It is assumed that individuals displaying rational behaviours try to maximise their economic benefits and that they continuously do cost-benefit analysis in the process of decision-making. Rational behaviours are associated with economic decisions, and it is thought that individuals can also behave rationally in other areas. It becomes possible with this approach to analyse political and cultural processes and also education as the design of individuals acting rationally. This form of analysis and description is the product of efforts which will ensure the formation of markets by using economic reasoning in all social domains. While individuals shape their behaviours according to criteria for economic activities on the one hand, they transform the society on the other. Thus, HCT has not only recommended a model to analyse the domain of education, but it also has transformed it according to economic rationality.

The content of education received today is largely regulated according to the requirements of global economy, and international organisations play active roles in this process. Rizvi and Lingard (2010) state that international organisations fulfilling several functions in the development of the conception of education for economy are becoming centres where education-related knowledge is regulated and that they develop discourses that educational reforms are made in accordance with the needs of global economy. Such discourse is shaped on the grounds that information and communication technologies develop, and therefore the qualifications for workforce change, that education should also be modified to meet the changing qualifications. The term 'knowledge economy' is used to describe the changes experienced in the economy and to emphasise the increasing importance of knowledge. The knowledge-economy approach, which might seem to be different from HCT, is based on a renewed HCT. The arguments put forward in this modern form of HCT can be said to be extended to contain not only individuals but also companies and governments. In this approach, which is based on description of rational individuals, it is argued that performance in a global economy is more and more dependent on individuals' accumulation of knowledge, their levels of skills, learning capacities and cultural adjustment. In contrast, while duration of schooling is not focused on very much in the contemporary form of HCT, an approach attaching importance to learning properties that individuals can develop so as to cope with the unknown and constantly-changing work conditions and aiming to develop human resources is adopted. While individuals develop human capital on the one hand, they have to renew the properties they develop according to changing economic conditions. Thus, investment in human capital is made continuously, not only once as in contemporary HCT.

HCT, which conceptualises education from the aspect of mainstream economy, ignores the cultural and social aspects of life in general and of education specifically; and if it does not ignore, it does this using reductionist models and uses terms of economy. Therefore, it considers the shaping of education on the basis of economy as an important function. The goals of education are described on the basis of raising the workforce needed by the economy, especially in recent years. While such a description causes a shrinking in the meaning of education, it makes considering it in a larger framework of rich practices and goals (Gillies, 2017). However, the objective of education is not only to meet the needs of the economy. Education is a process which ensures that students recognise and explore themselves and which prepares them for a democratic society. Therefore, conducting it in consistence with HCT and putting it to economic analysis results in several difficulties. Obstacles can be formed against disadvantaged sections of society for such reasons as inconsistency with economic rationality. As Gillies (2017) stresses, the disadvantaged groups, or those having learning difficulties, are considered as wasted investment opportunities – not as such values as justice, equality and moral – in HCT. It is probable that educational configuration and a social formation shaped by economic rationality will emerge by ignoring solutions outside the economy. Individuals thinking of others' good or acting on the basis of public good are not needed in this formation. Yet, humans are not creatures acting according to economic rationality – as considered in all these economic analyses. However, neoclassical economics and HCT assume that individuals act according to economic rationality, ensuring that this is generalised in all social domains.

Summary points

- HCT has an important part in the effects of economy on education and in describing the economic role of education.
- It is assumed that individuals invest in themselves through good quality education to make them well-qualified workforce to raise their income in the future, and that this investment, which leads to increase in productivity, results in economic growth.
- Economic analyses performed on the basis of HCT with the assumption of rational individuals isolated from social belongingness and accumulation of fictional knowledge made in this way lead to the economisation of education and thus to the transformation of educational processes on the basis of economic priorities.
- International organisations such as the OECD and the World Bank have important functions in spreading the conception of education for economy.
- HCT, which conceptualises education from the perspective of mainstream economy, ignores the cultural and social dimensions of life in general, and specifically; even though it does not ignore it, it expresses them in economic terms.

Recommended readings

Baptiste, I. (2001) Educating lone wolves: pedagogical implications of human capital theory. *Adult Education Quarterly*, 51(3), pp. 184–201.
Gilead, T. (2012) Rousseau, happiness, and the economic approach to education. *Educational Theory*, 62(3), pp. 267–285.
Robeyns, I. (2006) Three models of education: rights, capabilities and human capital. *Theory and Research in Education*, 4(1), pp. 69–84.

References

Althusser, L. (2006) *Ideolojive Devletin Ideolojik Aygıtları* (Trans. A. Tümertekin). Istanbul: Ithaki Yayınları.
Arrow, K.J. (1973) Higher education as a filter. *Journal of Public Economics*, 2(3), pp. 193–216.
Becker, G.S. (1964) *Human Capital: A Theoretical and Empirical Analysis, with Special Reference to Education*. New York: National Bureau of Economic Research.
Becker, G.S. (1993) *Human Capital: A Theoretical and Empirical Analysis, with Special Reference to Education* (3rd edition). Chicago and London: Chicago University Press.
Billington, R. (2003) *Living Philosophy: An Introduction to Moral Thought* (3rd edition). London: Routledge.
Blaug, M. (1976) The empirical status of human capital theory: a slightly jaundiced survey. *Journal of Economic Literature*, 14(3), pp. 827–855.
Blaug, M. (1985) Where are we now in the economics of education? *Economics of Education*, 4(1), pp. 17–28.
Bowles, S. and Gintis, S. (1975) The problem with human capital theory: a Marxian critique. *American Economic Review*, 65(2), pp. 74–82.
Bowles, S. and Gintis, S. (1976) *Schooling in Capitalist America: Educational Reform and the Contradictions of Economic Life*. New York: Basic Books.
Brown, W. (2015) *Undoing the Demos: Neoliberalism's Stealth Revolution*. New York: Zone Books.
Bugra, A. (1995) *Iktisatçılar ve Insanlar: Bir yöntem çalısması*. Istanbul: Iletisim Yayınları.
Cain, G.G. (1976) The challenge of segmented labor market theories to orthodox theories: a survey. *Journal of Economic Literature*, 14(4), pp. 1215–1257.

Denison, E. (1962) *The Sources of Economic Growth in the United States.* New York: Committee for Economic Development.
Ercan, F. and Uzunyayla, F. (2009) A class perspective on the new actors and their demands from the Turkish education system. In D. Hill and E. Rosskam (eds.), *The Developing World and State Education: Neoliberal Depredation and Egalitarian Alternatives.* New York: Routledge.
Foucault, M. (2008) *The Birth of Biopolitics: Lectures at the Collège de France.* (Trans. G. Burchell). New York: Palgrave Macmillan.
Gillies, D. (2017) Human capital theory in education. In M.A. Peters (ed.), *Encyclopedia of Educational Philosophy and Theory.* Singapore: Springer.
Gorz, A. (2001) *Yaşadığımız Sefalet: Kurtuluş çareleri* (Trans. N. Tutal). İstanbul: Ayrıntı Yayınları.
Kjelland, J. (2008) Economic returns to higher education: signaling v. human capital theory – an analysis of competing theories. *The Park Place Economist,* 16, pp. 70–77.
Lauder, H., Young, M., Daniels, H., Balarin, M. and Lowe, J. (2012) Introduction: educating for the knowledge economy? Critical perspectives. In H. Lauder, M. Young, H. Daniels, M. Balarin and J. Lowe (eds.), *Educating for the Knowledge Economy? Critical Perspectives.* London and New York: Routledge.
Marshall, A. (2013) *Principles of Economics* (8th edition). London: Palgrave Macmillan. (Original work published in 1890.)
Marx, K. (2011) *Kapital: 1. Cilt* (Trans. M. Selik & N. Satlıgan). İstanbul: Yordam Kitap (Original work published in 1890).
Mincer, J. (1958) Investment in human capital and personal income distribution. *Journal of Political Economy,* 66(4), pp. 281–302.
MoNE (2019) Avrupa Birliği ve Projeler Koordinasyon Daire Başkanlığı. Available at: https://abdigm.meb.gov.tr/www/projeler/icerik/930 (Accessed 30 May 2019).
OECD (2014) *Skills Beyond School: Synthesis Report, OECD Reviews of Vocational Education and Training.* Available at: www.oecd.org/education/skills-beyond-school/Skills-Beyond-School-Synthesis-Report.pdf (Accessed 15 May 2018).
Özsoy, S. (2002) Yükseköğretimde ticarileşme süreci ve hak söylemi. *Ozgür Universite Forumu,* 17, pp. 80–103.
Rizvi, F. and Lingard, B. (2010) *Globalizing Education Policy.* New York: Routledge.
Schultz, T.W. (1960) Capital formation by education. *Journal of Political Economy,* 68(6), pp. 571–583.
Schultz, T.W. (1961) Investment in human capital. *American Economic Review,* 51(1), pp. 1–17.
Sennett, R. (2006) *The Culture of the New Capitalism.* New Haven, CT: Yale University Press.
Smith, A. (1976) *An Inquiry into the Nature and Causes of the Wealth of Nations.* Chicago: University of Chicago Press. (Original work published in 1776.)
Spence, M. (1973) Job market signaling. *Quarterly Journal of Economics,* 87(3), pp. 355–374.
Spring, J. (2015) *Economization of Education: Human Capital, Global Corporations, Skill-Based Schooling.* New York: Routledge.
Tan, E. (2014) Human capital theory: a holistic criticism. *Review of Educational Research,* 84(3), pp. 411–445.
Unal, L.I. (1996) *Egitim ve Yetistirme Ekonomisi.* Ankara: Epar Yayınları.
Woodhall, M. (1987) Economics of education: a review in economics of education: Research and studies. In G. Psacharopoulos (ed.), *Economics of Education Research and Studies.* Oxford: Pergamon Press.
World Bank (2005) Education Sector Strategy update: achieving education for all, broadening our perspective, maximizing our effectiveness. Available at: http://siteresources.worldbank.org/EDUCATION/Resources/ESSU/Education_Sector_Strategy_Update.pdf (Accessed 15 February 2018).

7 Inequalities, precariousness and education

Schooling precarious workers

Brian McDonough

Introduction

This chapter examines the precarious nature of education in a neoliberal economy. Drawing on the work of Standing's (2015) *The Precariat: The New Dangerous Class*, and other Marxist thinkers, the chapter explores how education serves a rapidly ever-changing labour market, increasingly associated with insecurity, instability and poorly paid work. Driven by neoliberal interests, the education system in capitalist societies is characterised by tiered and separate schooling systems for the privileged elite and under-privileged social groups and social classes in society. The chapter argues that in an 'age of insecurity' (Sennett, 2006), education systems can often exacerbate social inequalities, with a tendency to mirror neoliberal labour markets and bow down to its needs and economic requirements. For most, schooling is no longer geared towards 'choosing a career', but preparing for a working-life characterised by insecurity and change in which casual labour and an uncertain future are typical life-course experiences. Precariousness not only affects those in typically 'working-class' or 'routine' jobs but also typically middle-class professions such as schoolteachers, university lecturers, and a whole range of professional occupations elsewhere. The chapter explores inequalities, precariousness, and education from at least three standpoints. First, it looks at the relationships between education, neoliberalism and the labour market, examining how schooling is shaped to fit the needs of a precariat labour market. Second, it looks at precariousness in education itself, highlighting the commodification of workers in the education sector, from supply teachers in secondary schools, to hourly-paid and zero-contracted lecturers in further and higher education sectors. Third, it looks at the commodification of education itself, particularly how HE has become market-led. Aside from these three approaches to understanding precariousness and education, the chapter also examines the 'gig economy' and the notion of the 'Edu-factory'.

Since the 1970s, the neoliberal model has dominated our thinking, with the central idea that market competitiveness will provide growth and development across societies. At the forefront of this model is the idea that 'everything should be done to maximize competition and competitiveness, and allow market principles to permeate all aspects of life' (Standing, 2015: 1). The ideas about how financial and social systems should work are rooted in a style of economics known as 'laissez-faire', literally meaning 'let the market rip' or 'let the market do as it pleases' (see Friedman, 1962). If the 'free market' is allowed to 'let rip' it will 'naturally' provide economic growth across entire communities, so the argument goes, spreading wealth wherever the market takes root and flourishes. But the neoliberal model provides winners and losers. As one market or industry expands, economic growth provides success for certain groups of people. But as the market crashes elsewhere, whole industries and communities can suffer from economic hardship and deprivation. Precariousness is just one side effect of the neoliberal model and relates to a plethora of other factors which impact upon social inequalities, including gender, ethnicity, social class, age, nationality, sexuality, disability and religion. This chapter draws upon some of these factors in order to better understand how neoliberal imperatives impact upon the nature and relationship between precariousness and education.

Schooling has been shaped by, and is subject to, political, economic and social interests. Henry Giroux (2011: 14) explains 'how classroom learning embodies selective values, is entangled with relations of power, entails judgements about what knowledge counts, legitimates specific social relations, defines agency in particular ways, and always presupposes a particular notion of the future'. Schooling cannot be separated from the political or economic ties of the social world. The schooling system, as part of a wider educational system, is a coercive force which provides both opportunities and limitations for individual lives. With the emergence of neoliberal economics, both education and the labour market have been reshaped, in some cases mirroring each other. This idea is nothing new. Since the 1970s, Marxists studying the role of education have examined this 'mirroring effect', describing how education directly reproduces the capitalist relations of production:

> The educational system helps integrate youth into the economic system, we believe, through a structural correspondence between its social relations and those of production. The structure of social relations in education not only inures the student to the discipline of the workplace, but develops the types of personal demeanor, modes of self-presentation, self-image, and social class identifications which are crucial ingredients of job adequacy. Specifically, the social relationships of education – the relationships between administrators and teachers, teachers and students, students and students, and students and their work – replicate the hierarchal division of labour.
>
> (Bowles and Gintis, 1976: 131)

This Marxist account of how inequality is reproduced within the education system suggests that what goes on in schools directly corresponds to the world of work. Education ensures that workers will adapt to the needs of the system, often without questioning or challenging it. Another key Marxist writer, Louis Althusser (1918–1990), described the ideological conditioning effects of the educational system. In *Essays on Ideology*, Althusser argued that education could be used as a tool of the ruling class, used to subjugate the proletariat (working classes) and maintain the status quo. More than forty years on, many of these Marxist arguments still have relevance today, but Guy Standing's (2015) notion of 'the precariat' provides a more nuanced account of the experiences that individuals (from varied classes and backgrounds) have in a neoliberal context. This chapter draws on some of these theorists and ideas to make sense of the ways in which schooling produces workers in a neoliberal context.

The chapter first outlines the nature of the precariat, precarious work and the emerging 'gig economy', defined as 'selling humans as service', but also ignoring 'traditional employment law protection' (Prassl, 2018: 4). It then looks at how the precariat is schooled in contemporary education systems. After examining the problems with precariousness, the chapter looks at ways in which education may provide a route to escaping precariousness and the prospects for precarious workers from varied ages, gender and disabilities. The final sections examine the commodification of education.

The precariat, precarious work and the 'gig economy'

One underlying theme and adverse side effect of the neoliberal model is that countries increase labour-market flexibility and from this results precariousness. The agenda for a neoliberal market is supported by 'transferring risks and insecurity onto workers and their families' (Standing, 2015: 1). The result of this, says Standing (2015: 1), 'is the creation of a global "precariat", consisting of many millions around the world without an anchor of stability'. Standing (2015: 11) defines the precariat as 'a distinctive socio-economic group' by drawing on notions of 'precariousness' and the Marxist concept of the 'proletariat'. The precariat's lifestyle is one of instability and change. As markets fluctuate, so does the needs for workers in certain industries, providing a pick-and-mix-world of human labour. The old-fashioned images of construction workers and dockers waiting in line to be called up for work is now not so outdated. Precarious work is as relevant today as ever before, but instead of standing in line on industrial sites, precarious workers queue up on websites. It might appear that 'digital platform workers are a new social class or that they do not belong to a class', yet 'the class conflict interests (wages, benefits, employment and working conditions, collective action) of digital platform workers are similar to other members of the working class' (Mutaner, 2018: 1).

These issues are accelerated by the characteristics of the 'gig economy', which describes a way of working that is based on having temporary jobs or doing separate pieces of work, each paid separately, rather than having one mainstream job and employer. Instead, individuals are increasingly encouraged to 'free' themselves from inflexible employers and contracts and 'become their own boss'. However, work is legally protected, entrepreneurship is not. Prassl (2018) refers to the gig economy as one of the most significant transformations of work, where work is rebranded as entrepreneurship and labour sold as a technology by big technology giants. Examples includes services such as postal work, ordering and delivering takeaway food, taxi work, graphic design and artwork, hospitality, care work, freelancing, and other labour service work. Caregiver jobs, for example, include looking after the elderly, babysitting or nanny work (see companies like Urban Sitter). There are even house-sitting and pet-sitting services (see companies like Rover) which exemplify the 'gig economy'. In the United States, delivery jobs include working for companies such as AmazonFlex, Door Dash and Postmates, all of which use temporary and/or self-employed workers to carry out their tasks. In the United Kingdom, food delivery companies such as Deliveroo provide shift workers with earnings per job, even asking their 'self-employed' workers to pay for their own equipment needed to work for them. In 2017, a Deliveroo worker went to a tribunal after being told to pay £60 for a backpack and insulating bag required for the job. The 21-year-old former worker, Nathaniel Shaugnessy, said: 'If anyone's equipment breaks after six months they are expected to work the equivalent of the next 13 deliveries for nothing, just for the privilege of having the kit to do the job' (Tims, 2017). There are many more companies like this in the gig economy. Upwork, an online and global marketplace for freelancers in areas of graphic design and web development, have workers on hourly or fixed-price earnings. Like many apps and companies in the gig economy, they charge their own fees for workers to access the marketplace and get in touch with 'employers'. This is much the same as Uber who take a fee from its drivers for every ride they take with a customer. As self-employed workers, Uber drivers have few legislative protections and little chance to establish trade unions which can challenge organisation, injustice or inequalities, including:

> the right for employers to pay for social security, disability and unemployment insurance; the right to sick pay; the right to maternity or paternity paid leave; retirement benefits; profit sharing plans and the right to offer protection from discrimination on the basis of race, ethnicity, religion, sex, age, sexuality, disability, or reports of sexual harassment or any other employer wrongdoing.
>
> (McDonough, 2017: 66)

Companies like Instagram (voted one of the highest-paid gig jobs of 2018) provide a space for marketing freelancers to run marketing campaigns, but again don't offer stable employment to these 'gig economy' workers. What they offer are platforms and online spaces in which the precariat can pick up work. Essentially, the precariat sells his or her labour, often living a piecemeal existence. As Marx (2007: 21) says in *Economic and Philosophic Manuscripts*, the 'worker has become a commodity and it is a bit of luck for him if he can find a buyer'. As markets continually fluctuate and are ever-changing, so the precariat moves from job to job, sometimes managing multiple jobs at the same time. Whilst this freedom of working in your own time seems to offer the opportunity to become a sole trader, self-employed, or entrepreneur, individuals are still working with very few benefits, and global technological giants enjoy huge margins of profit whilst regarding themselves as 'matchmakers and workers as independent entrepreneurs' (Prassl, 2018: 4).

At first sight, the neoliberal economy seems attractive to a variety of potential workers, offering a wide variety of ways in which workers can 'pick up' work and earn some sort of a living. But the neoliberal gig economy is the *wild west of economics* – there are cowboy companies (big and small) heavily exploiting gig economy workers, charging them for membership, equipment, or fees before they have even started work. Then there is the reality that workers in the gig economy get no holiday pay, sick leave, pension contributions, maternity or paternity pay, union membership, nor a whole range of fringe benefits companies traditionally provide. These are just some of the adverse side-effects for precarious workers and their families. The free-market economy can provide flexibility and 'choice', but can also create instability, gross inequality and exploitation.

Women are also particularly affected by precarious work and are disadvantaged in a multiplicity of ways in the gig economy. These disadvantages in work are still occurring, even at a time where girls in schools outperform boys across many subjects (Eden, 2017). First, women are more likely to find themselves in precarious employment due to the types of industry women typically work in. The 'feminisation' of work (Caraway, 2007) refers to whole sectors of industry which have been feminised bringing more women into the world of work. But on the whole, women still dominate the lowest paid and most precarious forms of employment, in low-paid clerical, catering, cleaning and cashiering work. Second, women are far from achieving gender equality; they continue to be marginalised, downgraded and exploited in the workplace in a variety of ways (Bolton and Muzio, 2008). Third, a gender-pay gap exists in every country around the globe, with women always paid significantly less (on average) than men. Women who step off a career ladder to care for their children, for example, 'may end up more exploited, having to do much uncompensated work-for-labour outside their paid hours' (Standing, 2015: 26). Very importantly, women typically have less job security than men and are less likely than men to be given promotion opportunities and career advancement. The gig economy does not improve any of these conditions since the jobs available in the gig economy are characterised by under-regulation; many jobs change rapidly with new technologies and digital platforms and so issues of harassment, underpaid work, gender-pay gaps and discrimination are not easily detectable (Fredrickson, 2015). With the rise of precarious work, either fuelled by the gig economy or collapsing industries and economic systems, the lives of working women need to be continually explored to address work inequalities.

Precarious employment is a worldwide trend, as acclaimed in Zimmermann's (2012) *The Precarious New World*, because neoliberalism is a global economics defined by relationships between countries all over the world. The core principle of neoliberalism is to let the markets dictate and reduce, as much as possible, any interference from the state. The Keynesian position is deeply frowned upon by free-market thinkers. In pursuing market efficiency, the labour markets of economies have become increasingly deregulated, and regulations which largely protect workers' interests are removed. Precarious employment involves instability, lack of protection, insecurity and social or economic vulnerability (McDonough, 2017). In Britain, there have been street demonstrations and protests over what is commonly known as 'zero-hours', 'McJobs' or 'Burger King' contracts (named after the fast-food chains infamous for employing low-skilled and low-paid jobs). Similar protests have also taken place in the United States, such as the *Occupy Wall Street* movement (Vono de Vilhena et al., 2016: 98), and in Spain, protests known as *Indignados* (Standing, 2015). The widespread discontent and contempt for precarious work is largely down to the fact that it cuts across traditional social-class boundaries and impacts upon workers from all sectors of industry, including hospitals, universities, schools and a wide range of both middle-class and working-class professions. The precariat, says Standing (2015: 22), 'is far from homogeneous'. The teenager, the migrant and the single mother have distinctive lives, yet all share a sense of precariousness.

The role of education and schooling in society is constantly shaped by different economic, political and cultural changes. The increasing diversification of the job market has developed alongside the digital revolution; this has added pressures onto education, aligning it closer to the needs of employers. Yet should education be so closely linked to the needs of the economy and employers? In the light of the unpredictability of work and employment, perhaps the role of education should be on developing resilience, critical skills and creativity.

Question for reflection

1. How is education to respond to the increasing insecurity around work that the precariat encounter?

Schooling the precariat for the precarious workforce

One question this chapter asks is: how can schooling prepare the precariat worker? The schooling of the precariat is an important part of precariousness because the 'gig economy' and the plethora of zero-hours, part-time and piecemeal-style jobs requires a constant multitalented workforce with the perseverance and willingness to work varied shifts, at short notice, with poor contract conditions, or sometimes no contract at all. Schooling the precariat requires providing the adequate knowledge and skills needed for a changing economy, as well as the necessary IT skills required to use a plethora of social media platforms and modern organisations. But the precariat must also be instilled with the right values and work ethic required for capitalist society. Schooling the precariat for a precarious workforce requires powerful social institutions, like the education system, fundamental for equipping the precariat with essential understanding.

With reference to the educational system, there are arguments linking the commodification of education and the restructuring of the world of work, streaming youth into the flexible labour system, based on 'a privileged elite, a small technical working class and a growing precariat' (Standing 2015: 123). Since the education industry is selling commodities, and most young people are not expected to get a permanent job in a professional career, there is an open marketplace for substandard qualifications sold to substandard workers. (Standing, 2015: 123) provides the example of a surf-loving teenager who went to Plymouth University to study 'surf science and technology' requiring compulsory surfing twice a week. Standing calls these dumbed-down degrees for dumbed-down workers. From this perspective, the education system is providing substandard qualifications for substandard workers, quite fitting for the production of a precarious workforce. Nothing like this is prevalent for the privileged elite who still embark on traditional qualifications leading to high-paying professional occupations.

In a capitalist system, the education system is key to 'programming' precariat workers with the right values for work. Althusser (1976) described the education system as a piece of Ideological State Apparatus, or equipment, used for controlling society through norms and values transmitted through education itself. Following his argument, education does not transmit a set of common values, but transmits ruling-class or capitalist values *disguised* as common values. From this perspective, the precariat is misguided in thinking that the education system is there to help; rather it maintains, legitimates and reproduces, generation after generation, class inequalities in power and wealth. The precariat, bottom of the social-class pyramid, is conditioned to work hard in order to get results, believing that both educational success and hard work will pay off. But it never does, because the precariat's misfortune is a direct result of the neoliberal model, which aims to maximise productivity and minimise costs. Unfortunately, the precariat is part of the cost, and as a commodity is also subject to being sold, removed or replaced.

The world of schooling has also become highly dependent on the statistics produced by schools since the new interpretation of success and effective schooling is synonymous with academic results. Although schools are not deliberately willing to overlook individual students' needs, school academic results and how these are tied to funding have made metrics absolutely paramount for schools to remain open. Metrics and statistics impact on everyday school life, class time is devoted to practice tests, teachers' pedagogy is replaced by prescriptive and repetitive exercises to ensure good test results, and the student voice is drowned in an environment where the importance of metrics prevails. These practices which affect education significantly have been described as a result of the 'tyranny of numbers', leading to 'curriculum alignment' and 'teaching to the test', a way of 'juking the stats', a way in which 'institutions are perverted as effort is diverted from the institution's true purpose (education) to meeting the metric targets on which its survival has come to depend' (Muller, 2018: 2). Similarly, these strict codes of instruction that schools have had to develop in order to produce good test results also stunt the development of critical skills in students, and reinforce a blind allegiance to authority which is learnt very insidiously at school.

These schooling conditions encourage the precariat to appear docile and accepting of precarity and, in many cases, unjust conditions and treatment.

Despite the exploitative conditions in which the precariat exists, the conditioning throughout school means that the precariat is always eager and ready to sell his or her labour. The 'work ethic' is one of the most valued ideals in capitalist society. Those who work have value. Those who do not work are valueless. The idea that everyone in society must work is itself a fictitious narrative spurred by a neoliberal discourse which is preoccupied with the importance of paid employment and the idea of inclusion in the labour market (Levitas, 2005). The result is that neoliberalism polarises the idea of the 'work ethic' with 'laziness' and 'contempt' (McDonough and Bustillos Morales, 2019: 32). The 'work ethic' infiltrates every corner of industrialised society, yet most people in society are either too young, too old, too sick or too rich to work. In school, children are driven to work hard, achieve high results and make every attempt to do well. Schooling provides the perfect environment to prepare the precariat class for the world of work. In his work, *Essays on Ideology*, Althusser (1976: 6) says:

> What do children learn at school? They go varying distances in their studies, but at any rate they learn to read, to write and to add – i.e. a number of techniques, and a number of other things as well, including elements (which may be rudimentary or on the contrary thoroughgoing) of 'scientific' or 'literary culture', which are directly useful in the different jobs in production (one instruction for manual workers, another for technicians, a third for engineers, a final one for higher management, etc.).

Fifty years after Althusser was writing, many of the types of job may have changed, but the different categories still exist. The education system produces certain types of individuals conditioned into particular labour-power relations: learning to accept authority and so on. The labour system today differs, because after the growth of the knowledge economy and the coming and going of various financial crises, traditional forms of class relations and corresponding jobs in the labour market are blurred, and a 'new dangerous class' called the 'precariat' has emerged (Standing, 2015). The organisation of education is structured to benefit a fluctuating labour system, with selective (private and public) schooling for the privileged elite and other schooling for the small technical working classes and a growing precariat. More important than the knowledge and skills for production, described in the quote above, are the rules of good behaviour:

> But besides these techniques and knowledges, and in learning them, children also learn the rules of good behaviour, i.e. the attitude that should be observed by every agent in the division of labour, according to the job he is 'destined' for: rules of morality, civic and professional conscience, which actually means rules of respect for the socio-technical division of labour and ultimately the rules of the order established by class domination.
> (Althusser, 1976: 6)

Today we must also include in Althusser's analysis the position of the precariat who must learn the attitude and values in preparation for precarious work. Althusser (1976: 6–7) says that:

> the reproduction of labour-power requires not only a reproduction of its skills, but also, at the same time, a reproduction of its submission to the ruling ideology for the workers, and a

reproduction of the ability to manipulate the ruling ideology correctly for the agents of exploitation and repression, so that they, too, will provide for the domination of the ruling class.

Whilst the precariat must generally accept the poor prospects of living in a neoliberal world, Standing's (2015) conception of the precariat also shows the realisation of living in a dissatisfied and discontented world, evidenced by marches, protests and anti-establishment actions taken all over the world.

Question for reflection

1. Discuss whether you think schooling serves the needs of individuals or the needs of society?

Escaping precariousness through education?

In a world where education has become such an important part of everyday social life, questions need to be asked about its role in society, questions in relation to whether education and schooling nurture and open up opportunities for individuals, or whether education merely reproduces societal patterns, including its inequalities. Systems of education and schooling have become compulsory: all children must go to school to learn various skills and acquire the knowledge a society deems important. So it is important to explore whether our present systems of education help increase the chances of escaping precariousness?

Both Marx (2007) and Althusser (1976) argue that the world of education and schooling in society is primarily tying the individual to the labour market. There is little scope to see how workers can individually manage themselves out of exploitative conditions. A similar fate has been given to the precariat, whose ability to find work often 'depends on the whim of the rich and the capitalists' (Marx, 2007: 3). But some scholars have examined accounts in which education has made a difference to those in precarious work. They have asked: In what ways might new or higher qualifications benefit the precariat? Can education provide a route out of precariousness? One assumption is that educational qualifications should lead to higher productivity (Vono de Vilhena, et al., 2016) and therefore educational qualifications are associated with positive labour-market returns. The Organisation for Economic Co-operation and Development (OECD, 2002) found a '60 per cent higher rate of temporary employment for individuals who did not complete upper secondary education in comparison to their more educated counterparts' (Vono de Vilhena et al., 2016: 98). This indicates an association between educational level and reduced precariousness. There is also evidence that the chances of moving into permanent employment is lower for less-educated workers (Kalleberg, 2011; Vono de Vilhena et al., 2016), suggesting that the precariat ought to seek more educational qualifications in order to find permanent work, thus escaping precariousness. Some see temporary-style contracts of employments as probationary, leading to permanent contracts of employment. This is common in academia, where postgraduate students 'pick up' some hourly-paid teaching hours (usually on zero-hours contracts) before 'moving on' to permanent lectureships on completion of their doctorate. Gash (2008: 2) calls this idea a 'bridge', where precarious work is a temporary link, or transition, to a permanent contract. But Gash also shows how some precarious employment can constitute a 'trap' in some careers, questioning the role of education in the transition to 'better' positions. For example, in cases where temporary workers are used to fill short-term positions, such as staff absences and maternity leave, there are few opportunities for upward progression. For some precarious workers, a succession of temporary jobs can be all too common, with no end in sight to permanent and 'properly paid' work. In such situations temporary work is a 'trap' rather than a 'bridge'.

In some jobs, the pursuit of further training and education is much more of a tick-box exercise than having any real impact on job security, income or type of contract received. The precariat fills up 'spare time' with training and courses, often self-funded. Given the fierce competition, the precariat knows full well that to stand out in the marketplace, he or she will require the qualifications of others and more. Training and qualifications might have little effect on income or job security, but can often help provide an enhanced CV or give additional letters after one's name, making the costs of the course seem all worthwhile. One feature of precariatisation is called 'uptitling', whereby new job titles are created to recruit more qualified workers, yet they still work under precarious conditions (Standing, 2015: 29). This term specifically refers to the high-sounding epithet or title which helps conceal precariat tendencies. People are branded with titles like 'executive'; 'manager', 'director' and a whole range of other fancy bynames to give an illusion that there is more importance in what they do. But the 'con' neither tricks the precariat, nor leads them out of precariousness. The International Association of Administrative Professionals (the US occupational body) reported job titles such as 'front-office coordinator', 'electronic document specialist', 'media distribution officer' (paper boy/girl), 'recycling officer' (bin emptier) and 'sanitation consultant' (lavatory cleaner) (Standing, 2015: 29–30). Unfortunately, the job-title does not increase the pay, nor does it improve the conditions of employment. Whilst securing qualifications can make you more competitive in the complex world of work, work conditions still need to improve for individuals to reap the benefits of their educational achievements.

A system of compulsory education has also means that young people are encouraged to pursue academic qualifications. However, the system becomes an introduction to debt as individuals move through the educational system. A young precariat will often have to take on large debts if they are to study in further and higher education; but 'many find the jobs they can obtain are temporary and the wages too low to pay off those debts' (Standing, 2015: 126). Over the years that follow, the young precariat will have to take on jobs which do not fit with their qualifications and aspirations, which in itself can lead to 'status discord' and 'status frustration' in which 'people with a relatively high level of formal education' have to 'accept jobs that have a status or income beneath what they believe accord with their qualifications' (Standing, 2015: 16). As the precariat gets older, other limitations emerge, such as the collapse of industries or sectors which had once provided a source of decent income. Some older workers, having dedicated their working-life to one sector or another, find it difficult to turn their hands to new industries. The same difficulty to find new work, or upskill, can be said for workers whose job is replaced or automated by new technologies. For those older workers to take part in adult learning, the chances to find non-precarious employment can improve (Blanden et al., 2012; McMullin and Kilpi-Jakonen, 2014). So too can the increased earning potential of those adult learners who reskill in new industries (Vono de Vilhena et al., 2016). For those with impairments or 'disabilities', precariousness is heightened because the 'disabled' are more easily labelled as such and are swept to one side. Employers are reluctant to recruit those with an 'impaired performance' (Standing, 2015: 149). At the same time, as countries seek to maximise employment levels and minimise welfare spend, re-medicalising disability has made more of the disabled 'employable'. This has led to more disabled people joining the precariat population.

It seems that a system of education that has become so aligned with the needs of employers, and which has been redirected towards securing employment, is not halting the rise of the precariat. At a time where economic recessions have hit, and there are deep political troubles such as Brexit, more qualifications do not necessarily lead to better employment or better work conditions. There are many economic, cultural and social dynamics which are shaping the precariat, and education cannot be over-estimated, as it has become deeply bound up with the needs of society and the needs of the economy. Should our education systems continue to serve these economic and social needs so blindly? What are the changes needed to our education so that we can nurture individuals who are more critically aware of the external forces shaping the precariat? Are education and schooling the only answer to challenging the conditions suffered by the precariat? In seeking answers these questions we are required to think more openly about what the goals and aims of education and schooling should be.

The commodification and corporatisation of education and the edu-factory

The neoliberal forces creep into every facet of education, and so the privatisation and commercialisation of education are part and parcel of the neoliberal project. The university has become a 'knowledge factory' (Aronowitz, 2001) or 'edu-factory' in which courses are commodities to be sold for the highest price. In the United Kingdom, as in the United States and elsewhere, degrees are sold at high prices. Parents can pay up front, otherwise students will take out government-backed student loans or personal bank loans (often both) to fund their education. Standing (2015: 120) argues that 'commodifying higher education legitimises irrationality'. Any course offered at university is deemed acceptable if there is demand for it, providing that there are consumers willing to pay the price. The Taxpayers Alliance in 2007 identified some 401 'non-courses', including a degree in 'outdoor adventure with philosophy' at University College Plymouth St Mark and St John, and a degree in 'lifestyle management' at Leeds Metropolitan University. A higher education system driven by markets threatens traditional academic courses and disciplines, whilst still not guaranteeing that market-led courses will have any use in the changing world of employment.

The commodification of universities, whereby knowledge becomes a packaged, simplified and ready-to-be-sold product facilitates the conditions that make the precariat possible. The conditions that characterise the precariat are also an attack on democracy and the role education could have in maintaining democratic values in society. Giroux refers to education as being 'under attack' and argues that there is a 'realignment of the mission of HE within the discourse and ideology of the corporate world. Undermined as a repository of critical thinking, writing, teaching and learning, universities are refashioned to meet the interests of commerce and regulation' (Giroux, 2011: 52). Thus, once the process of education is reduced to market trends and customer satisfaction, the nature of the institution becomes subservient to satisfying the needs of a globalised capitalist reality. Giroux explains this by saying:

the mission of the university becomes instrumental … this means privileging instrumental over substantive knowledge, shifting power away from faculty to administrators, and corporatizing the culture of the university. As the college curriculum is stripped of those subjects (typically in the humanities) that do not translate immediately into market considerations, programs are downsized and reduced to service programs for business. In this case, not only does instrumental knowledge replace substantive knowledge as the basis for research, writing and teaching, but the university intellectual is reduced to low-level technocrat whose role is to manage and legitimate the downsizing, knowledge production, and labor practices that characterize the institutional power and culture of the corporatized and vocationalized university.

(Giroux, 2011: 52)

The corporatisation of the university is a half-way house to full privatisation. They use management models of corporate organisations, but the company's shares still remain in the ownership of the state and are not privately owned, nor shared or sold on the stock market. The corporatisation of the university has radically changed the educational environment for both staff and students alike. Nearly everything, including both learning and thinking, becomes objectified – reduced to metrics on the National Student Survey (NSS) – understood and managed by administrators using target-driven indicators. Academics are given a range of administrative titles which reflect this corporate shift. This might include becoming an 'Admissions Tutor', responsible for getting suitable students firmly placed on the course, or spending time in the summer working on the admissions 'hot desks'. The focus on 'driving sales' has seen a surge in academics engaged with schools and colleges – drumming up business by performing guest lectures; masterclass workshops, taster days, summer schools and a range of other recruitment activities that thirty years ago an academic would not have been obliged to participate in. 'Course Leaders' create strategies for making the degree attractive and marketable, posing for online videos and talking at open-day fairs. They also create strategies for moving up the various league tables, including initiatives to improve in the NSS. At many universities, academics are tasked with a wide range of administrative tasks, from entering student marks to attending to spreadsheets. Since 2017, British universities have also been subject to the government imposed Teaching Excellence Framework (TEF), in which they are ranked gold, silver or bronze according to various assessments. As a consequence of the ranking system, HE has become even more target-driven and performance-related. The focus is not on education *per se*, but how to move up the rankings by improving on each of the metrics used to score the institution (Muller, 2018).

Conclusion

This chapter examined the precarious nature of education in a neoliberal economy. Drawing on Standing's (2015) idea of the precariat, the chapter explored how education serves a rapidly ever-changing labour market. Standing shows how precariousness not only affects those in typically 'working-class' or 'routine' jobs, but also typically middle-class professions such as schoolteachers, university lecturers, and a whole range of professional occupations in education and elsewhere. He argues that education systems are commodified and restructured to stream youth into the flexible labour system. The 'new' structures involve a privileged elite, small technical working class and a growing precariat. Since the majority of young people are not expected to get a permanent job in a professional career, there is a market for substandard qualifications sold to substandard workers.

The chapter also uses Althusser's ideas about ideology, in so far as they made sense of how the precariat is schooled. Education provides the precariat not only with knowledge and skills but also the right values and attitudes required for a capitalist 'work ethic'. Althusser's Marxism is self-deterministic: the proletariat is conditioned in school (and elsewhere) and is always and already subject to the forces of production, readily exploited in the labour market. But Standing's precariat provides a more nuanced approach to exploitative conditions in a contemporary neoliberal context: far from being ideologically attuned to accept conditions, the precariat is deeply unsatisfied, and precariousness has become an issue all over the world. In Spain, for example, there are continual debates about *precariedad laboral* (precarious labour), or on *trabajo temporal* (temporary employment). In Germany, the debate revolves around the *Erosion der Normalarbeitsverhaltnisse* (erosion of collectively regulated employment), whilst in the United Kingdom, there is constant political debate over 'zero-hours' contracts (or Burger King contracts). There is resistance against precariousness, which is why Standing (2015: 1) describes the precariat as 'the new dangerous class'.

The chapter showed that schooling is no longer about 'picking a career', but preparing for a working-life characterised by insecurity and instability. New possibilities for education are needed, together with a more critical stance towards aligning education and schooling so closely to employment and the demands of industry. The chapter also discusses how precarious workers are made by societal dynamics, and are not just a product of the choices individuals make in their education and employment. The reflexivity of the precariat to improving their lives can only go hand in hand with the opportunities that exist in society to do that.

Summary points

- The precariat is a notion used to explain the new and rapidly changing insecurities and precarious working and living conditions that are faced by people in society. These precarities were once mainly experienced by those who were unemployed or unqualified; yet, in recent times the precariat can also be employed, educated and highly qualified.
- Making education and schooling more aligned with the needs of employers shapes students to accept precarious conditions in the workplace and not to challenge authority in the face of injustice.
- Whilst participating in education and acquiring qualifications were once seen as a way to secure steady and well-remunerated employment, precarious conditions are experienced by those who have pursued traditional educational routes, such as university.
- The corporatisation and commodification of schools and universities facilitate precarious conditions experienced by the precariat. Knowledge is simplified, criticality is discouraged and the rationality of employers and capitalist structures becomes normalised and unquestionable.

Recommended readings

Ball, S.J. (2012) *Global Education Inc.: New Policy Networks and the Neoliberal Imaginary*. Abingdon: Routledge.
Kessler, S. (2019) *Gigged: The Gig Economy, the End of the Job and the Future of Work*. London: Penguin Books.

References

Althusser, L. (1976) *Essays on Ideology*. London: Verso.
Aronowitz, S. (2001) *The Knowledge Factory: Dismantling the Corporate University and Creating True Higher Education*. Boston: Beacon Press.
Blanden, J., Buscha, F., Sturgis, P. and Urwin, P. (2012) Measuring the earning returns to lifelong learning in the UK. *Economics of Education Review*, 31(4), pp. 501–514.
Bolton, S. and Muzio, D. (2008) The paradoxical processes of feminisation in the professions: the case of established, aspiring and semi-professions. *Work, Employment and Society*, 22(2), pp. 281–299.
Bowles, S. and Gintis, H. (1976) *Schooling in Capitalist America: Educational Reform and the Contradictions of Economic Life*. London: Routledge and Kegan Paul.
Caraway, T.L (2007) *Assembling Women: The Feminization of Global Manufacturing*. Ithaca, NY: Cornell University Press.
Eden, C. (2017) *Gender Education and Work: Inequalities and Intersectionality*. London: Routledge.
Fredrickson, C. (2015) *Under the Bus: How Working Women Are Being Run Over*. London: The New Press.
Friedman, M. (1962) *Capitalism and Freedom*. Chicago: University of Chicago Press.
Gash, V. (2008) Bridge or trap? Temporary workers' transitions to unemployment and to the standard employment contract. *European Sociological Review*, 24(5), pp. 651–668.
Giroux, H.A. (2011) *On Critical Pedagogy*. London: Bloomsbury.
Kalleberg, A. (2011) *Good Jobs, Bad Jobs: The Rise of Polarized and Precarious Employment Systems in the United States 1970s to 2000s*. New York: Russell Sage Foundation.
Levitas, R. (2005) *The Inclusive Society? Social Exclusion and New Labour*. Basingstoke: Palgrave Macmillan.
Marx, K. (2007) *Economic and Philosophic Manuscripts of 1844*. New York: Dover Publications.
McDonough, B. (2017) Work and unemployment. In S. Isaacs (ed.), *Social Problems in the UK: An Introduction*. Abingdon: Routledge.
McDonough, B. and Bustillos Morales, J. (2019) *Universal Basic Income*. London: Routledge.
McMullin, P. and Kilpi-Jakonen, E. (2014) Cumulative (dis)advantage? Patterns of participation and outcomes of adult learning in Great Britain. In H.P. Blossfeld, E. Kilpi-Jakonen, D. Vono de Vilhena and S. Buchholz (eds.), *Adult Learning in Modern Societies: An International Comparison from a Life-course Perspective*. Cheltenham: Edward Elgar.
Muller, J. (2018) *The Tyranny of Metrics*. Princeton, NJ: Princeton University Press.
Mutaner, C. (2018) Digital platforms, gig economy, precarious employment, and the invisible hand of social class. *International Journal of Health Services*, 48(4), pp. 597–600.
OECD (2002) *Organisation for Economic Co-operation and Development: Taking the Measure of Temporary Employment*. In OECD (eds.), Employment Outlook 2002. Paris: OECD, pp. 127–185.
Prassl, J. (2018) *Humans as Service: The Promise and Perils of Work in the Gig Economy*. Oxford: Oxford University Press.
Sennett R. (2006) *The Culture of the New Capitalism*. New Haven, CT: Yale University Press.
Standing, G. (2015) *The Precariat: The New Dangerous Class*. London: Bloomsbury.
Tims, A. (2017) Gig economy ruling has Deliveroo riders without rights and buying their own kit. *The Guardian*, 19 November 2017. Available at: www.theguardian.com/business/2017/nov/19/gig-economy-ruling-deliveroo-riders-equipment-basic-employment-rights (Accessed 19 November 2017).
Vono de Vilhena, D., Kosyakova, Y., Kilpi-Jakonen, E. and McMullin, P. (2016) Does adult education contribute to securing non-precarious employment? A cross-national comparison. *Work, Employment and Society*, 30(1), pp. 97–117.
Zimmermann, K.F. (2012) The precarious new world of informal jobs. *Harvard Business Review*. Available at: https://hbr.org/2012/11/a-precarious-new-world-of-info (Accessed 15 July 2019).

8 The economics of the university
Knowledge, the market and the state

Stephen Ward

Introduction

In recent years, universities in the United Kingdom have been in the news, attracting public attention to their finances with political debates about student fees and vice-chancellors' salaries (Adams and Gamper, 2018). HE in the United Kingdom is a flourishing business with in 2016 an overall surplus of £33bn. It is the only public sector which, between 2010 and 2018, did not suffer the effects of the financial 'austerity' policy which the Coalition and Conservative governments imposed on public finances following the 2008 banking crisis and budgetary deficit. During those years universities continued to expand, spending capital on new buildings and staff. That universities have enjoyed such status in society derives perhaps from their traditions and longevity. Beginning in Europe in the eleventh century, universities have a history of nearly a millennium and it is interesting to reflect that, apart from the church, the university predates other social institutions like schools, banks and hospitals.

This chapter takes a historical perspective on the economic theories which have underpinned HE over three broad phases: the medieval, the modern and the postmodern. It examines the ways in which funding and governance, which themselves reflect changing political and economic ideologies, affect the structure of universities and the nature of university knowledge. It examines the changing relationship between university, society and the state. While universities still have a high level of independence compared with schools, we will see an erosion of university academic freedom through a mixture of government regulation and market forces.

The main focus of the chapter is the economics of HE in England and Wales. At the end of the twentieth century successive UK governments abandoned the post-war Keynesian economics of government investment and ownership of industry. The dominant political paradigm of neoliberal free-market economics framed government policy in all areas. For HE in England and Wales it made universities competitors in a market, students becoming consumers paying fees for the 'commodities' of knowledge and qualifications. Until the 1960s university education in the United Kingdom was for an intellectual elite of only five per cent of the population. The expansion of universities and subsequent policies of 'widening participation' have led to mass higher education with almost 50 per cent of the 18–30 population now gaining access to university education. Despite the annual fees of £9,250 in 2018, a university education is a highly valued 'commodity' among young people, their parents and employers.

> **Questions for reflection**
>
> 1. HE is now an expensive business. Many people give up earning money in the short term and pay university fees. What are their reasons for doing this?
> 2. What made you decide to go into HE?

Medieval origins of the university

Our main concern is the recent political and economic changes which have placed universities in the market, but the medieval period is worth looking at to see some surprising similarities to subsequent models of HE. There are some obvious vestiges of the medieval in universities today. They all like to recall their medieval and liturgical origins with chancellors, vice chancellors, professors, deans, masters and honours degrees. They indulge in graduation ceremonies with processions decked out with the academic regalia of hoods, gowns, bedel and mace. These may be just the superficial trappings designed to impress and to stress their traditionalism, but they are a symptom of the market appeal to tradition.

The first European universities were in Paris, Bologna and Oxford in the eleventh century, and universities opened in the main cities across Europe. The medieval universities were autonomous institutions funded by student fees and endowments, some of which came via the Roman Catholic Church. Endowments by the wealthy were a key feature of funding. For example, New College Oxford founded by William Wykham in 1379 is one of the wealthiest colleges in Oxford; in 2017 it had financial endowments of over £243m and assets of over £286m (New College Oxford, 2017).

While the wealthy and the church were responsible for funding, they had little control over the day-to-day governance of the universities. The management of the colleges was in the hands of the 'masters' who did the teaching and exercised their authority. This independence of governance is a continuing feature of the university, as will be shown below in the section on the modern university. It is important to recognise that there was little or nothing in the way of what we now call 'state' funding for the medieval university. Funding came in various forms from the wealthy, and many students were the children of the wealthy. However, endowments allowed the universities to admit the sons of the poor or less wealthy, giving some attempts at equality of opportunity. Wealthy students provided funding through fees which were made directly to the master; students could pick and choose their masters and whose lectures they wished to attend, an early form of today's market forces.

In the medieval period national boundaries were fairly porous and, with Latin as a *lingua franca*, there was a high level of international communication among Europe's academic intellectuals. Awards were 'portable' in that students could attend different universities with credits from previous study (Toswell, 2017).

The modern university

The 'modern' university began with the Enlightenment and the industrial revolution. The politician Wilhelm von Humboldt established the University of Berlin in 1810 and Berlin became the model for the modern university in Europe. The state fully funds the university and gives it academic freedom to carry out research, to create knowledge and to teach: 'The university became a *privileged* place where the future of society is forged through research' (Haddad, 2000: 32). Berlin was the first university to provide the highly educated professionals required by industry and civil administration in exchange for freedom from the state and autonomy in the knowledge it produces. This was a massive change to both the politics and the financing of HE. The economic model of HE was essentially 'Keynesian': the state invests on behalf of the taxpayer. Private funding was taken out of the equation.

The philosophical concept of the modern university derives from nineteenth century German idealism, notably the work of Immanuel Kant. For Kant (1992) the basis of the university is reason, in contrast to superstition and tradition: '… a perpetual conflict between established tradition and rational enquiry' (Readings, 1996: 57). Kant does not see the university as divorced from culture and society, but he strikes a balance between the autonomy of reason and the power of the state. He argues that the role of the university is to produce technicians for the state – men of affairs. Humboldt employed Kant's notion of creating and sustaining a national culture through reasoned critique in the University of Berlin. Humboldt argued that 'the state protects the actions of the university; the university safeguards the thoughts of the state. And each strives to realise the idea of a national culture' (Readings, 1996: 69). The modern university is a means of the realisation of state nationalism, culture and identity. Humboldt's genius was to create a system in which the state finances the university, while ensuring autonomy for the institution and academic freedom for its teachers.

Another way of characterising the idea of academic freedom is in the famous book by Cardinal Newman (1996), *The Idea of a University.* Newman, writing in the mid-nineteenth century, suggests that university knowledge should be 'useless knowledge' as against the 'useful knowledge' required by employment and industry.

Question for reflection

1. Do you agree with the Humboldt university model, or should governments have more control and accountability for tax-payers' money?

Europe and the Bologna Process

Attempts at the end of the twentieth century to harmonise HE across Europe reflect the borderless quality of medieval universities. But it also defined the purpose of the modern university and its principles of academic freedom and the independence of economic and political control. The Bologna Process comprised a series of meetings to ensure comparability in the standards and quality of higher education qualifications. The first was the *Magna Charta Universitatum* (1988), signed at a meeting of European university rectors to celebrate the 900th anniversary of the University of Bologna. Its four principles are:

1. The university is an autonomous institution at the heart of societies differently organised because of geography and historical heritage. … To meet the needs of the world around

it, its research and teaching must be morally and intellectually independent of all political authority and economic power.
2. Teaching and research in universities must be inseparable if their tuition is not to lag behind changing needs, the demands of society, and advances in scientific knowledge.
3. Freedom in research and training is the fundamental principle of university life, and governments and universities, each as far as in them lies, must ensure respect for this fundamental requirement.
4. A university is the trustee of the European humanistic tradition; its constant care is to attain universal knowledge; to fulfil its vocation it transcends geographical and political frontiers, and affirms the vital need for different coloured cultures to know and influence each other.

Signed in 1997 the *Lisbon Recognition Convention* stipulates that degrees and periods of study are recognised across different countries, thus ensuring the 'portability' that had been a feature of the medieval university.

In 1998 the *Paris Sorbonne Declaration* was signed by the ministers of France, Germany, the United Kingdom and Italy to create a common frame of reference in a European Higher Education Area, where mobility should be promoted both for students and graduates, as well as for the teaching staff.

In 1999 the *Bologna Declaration* was agreed by 29 countries with the agreement to:

- a system of easily readable and comparable degrees with common terminology and standards;
- a system based on two main cycles, undergraduate and graduate, access to the second cycle [graduate education] requiring successful completion of first cycle lasting a minimum of three years.

However, Collini (2018: 1) protests that, while the United Kingdom signed up to the treaties in the Bologna Process, universities in Britain do not have the independence from political and economic interference enjoyed by others in Europe: '"An autonomous institution"? Barely a month goes by without a new diktat issuing from Whitehall and its satellite agencies. Governance is as constrained as policy' (2018: 1). The next section examines the ways in which the academic principles of the modern university have been eroded in the United Kingdom, and particularly in England and Wales.

The postmodern university: the state and the market

In 1963 the Robbins Commission (Committee on Higher Education, 1963) recommended the expansion of HE in Britain with the creation of more chartered universities and higher education in the colleges and polytechnics. The policy created the so-called 'binary divide' between universities with a royal charter and polytechnics and colleges controlled by the local education authorities (LEA). Anthony Crosland, Labour Secretary of State for Education in 1965, set up the system with the ambition of creating separate but equal branches of HE to serve different purposes. There would be the twin virtues of academic independence for the existing universities and, for the new polytechnics, local accountability and an emphasis on applied knowledge for industry.

Although the binary system permitted some financial independence for the polytechnics and colleges, it saw distinctly different forms of academic control between the two types of institution. The established universities with their royal charters were largely self-determining in their curriculum and assessment, while the polytechnics and colleges was rigorously controlled by the Council for National Academic Awards (CNAA). This was a government-funded organisation which operated to ensure the implementation of strict guidelines for curriculum structure, content and methods. Degree courses to be taught in the polytechnics were to be approved by the council and were required to meet all its criteria. Although it employed higher education 'peers' to implement its directives, it exercised a high level of control over higher education knowledge with rigorous scrutiny (Silver, 1990). The existence of this body signified the relationship of the institutions to the state. While the chartered universities enjoyed the Humboldt model with the trust of the state to define and codify knowledge, the polytechnics and colleges were under its watchful eye, with every item of knowledge rigorously audited and approved or rejected.

Freedom from local authority control was granted by the Education Secretary of State, Kenneth Baker, in 1989 with incorporation of polytechnics as independent financial institutions, but the request for university title as 'Polytechnic Universities' was refused. However, things were to change rapidly in 1991 with the new Secretary of State, Kenneth Clarke, who was reported to have said, 'Let's take the great plunge and make them all universities, let's get rid of all the arguments' (Kogan and Hanney, 2000: 139). With that the binary system was abolished at a stroke.

While this might appear to foreshadow an increase in independence for the higher education institutions, the outcomes were not so simple. The end of the twentieth century brought the New Right in British politics with neoliberal economic theory and a determination to rid the nation of Keynes's economic model of high taxation and state monopoly. It brought a different view of the management of public organisations and the professions. These are characterised as New Public Management (NPM) in 'the evaluative state' (Henkel, 1991). NPM is intended on the one hand to devolve power to institutions, but on the other to retain central control in order to reduce the power of professional bodies which is depicted as 'professional hegemony'. Margaret Thatcher's 1980s reforms were supposedly intended to roll back the state in 'a shift from academic control towards both the market and to the incorporation of universities in the generality of state control' (Henkel, 1991: 55). Readings (1996) sees the move as part of a larger process of converting the whole British university system into the neoliberal 'excellence' model to imitate the United States. The conversion of polytechnics into universities, he argues, was not an ideological commitment to expanding HE as such, but a mechanism to bring all institutions into the same competitive market in which the successful – as measured by the performance indicators – are rewarded by higher grant allocations.

This marks the move towards government control through market forces, or more particularly, the use of government controls to enable a free market: not a magnanimous egalitarian gesture towards the polytechnics, but an example of pure Thatcherism. Gray (1998) helps to explain this apparent contradiction in Conservative government policy where 'rolling back the state' appears to mean the removal of government controls, but which actually involves controls on institutions through nationally prescribed curricula and criteria. Gray maintains that the strong government intervention is always required to enable a free market, pointing out:

> Encumbered markets are the norm in every society, whereas free markets are a product of artifice, design and political coercion. *Laissez-faire* must be centrally planned: regulated markets

just happen. The free market is not, as New Right thinkers have imagined or claimed, a gift of social evolution. It is an end-product of social engineering and unyielding political will.

(1988: 17)

Readings argues that the very foundations of the traditional Western university are crumbling in postmodern chaos. The hollowing out of the nation state through global capitalism and transnational corporations led to the ruin of the modern university, for the primacy of the nation-state is in the role of the university:

> The modern university was conceived by Humboldt as one of the primary apparatuses through which this production of national subjects was to take place in modernity, and the decline of the nation-state raises serious questions about the nature of the contemporary function of the university.
>
> (1996: 46)

Question for reflection

1. The binary higher education system in Britain was designed to create universities providing 'academic' degrees and polytechnics providing vocational studies. Do you agree with the principle of there being two types of university: those which teach purely 'academic' subjects such as philosophy, the arts and humanities, and those which teach 'vocational' subjects such as engineering and teaching?

Performativity

A key feature of the postmodern university is 'performativity': universities are judged on the extent to which they prepare their students for employment. For Readings, 'culture' is no longer the watchword of the university:

> The university is no longer Humboldt's, and that means it is no longer *The* university. The Germans not only founded a University and gave it a mission; they also made the University into the decisive instance of intellectual activity. All of this is in the process of changing: intellectual activity and the culture it revived are being replaced by the pursuit of excellence and performance indicators.
>
> (1996: 55)

The expansion of HE changes the original role of the university which was to educate an intellectual elite. It must now engage with a broader range of the population (50 per cent of the 18–30 cohort). However, while policies of expansion and widening participation have been effective in terms of the sheer numbers in HE, British universities still operate within a highly selective basis which disadvantages working-class applicants. While the binary system was abolished in name, the pre-92 chartered universities have guarded their higher esteem and succeeded in maintaining their status with the typically British elite *Russell Group*. They are 24 self-proclaimed high-quality institutions, named because their vice-chancellors first met in the Russell Hotel, London (Which? University, 2018). The Sutton Trust (2018) finds, for example, that in 2015–2017 access to Russell

Group Universities was biased towards middle-class applicants, and that Oxbridge Universities took more applicants from eight independent (public) schools than from 2,800 state schools.

Tuition fees and the failed market

To strengthen competitive market forces in HE in 2005 Blair's New Labour government introduced 'variable' university tuition fees with a maximum of £3,000. The theory was that the 'best' universities (the Mercedes and BMWs) would be able to charge the higher fees, while the lesser ones (the Fords and the Fiats) would charge less. Because the demand for HE was so high, all apart from two charged the maximum fee and so the attempt to introduce market competition failed. At the time there was bitter opposition among Labour MPS to the introduction of fees. Blair's attempt to introduce the necessary legislation almost led to his government losing the vote in the house. The limit of £3,000 was a symptom of the government's weakness in not being able to introduce a proper competitive market; again, as Gray (1998) notes, strong government is needed to establish a market.

Universities complained that the £3,000 fee did not give sufficient income to provide high-quality education. The Browne Report (2010) on the funding of HE commissioned by the Labour government proposed a maximum fee of £6,000, which was the estimated cost of teaching. There was also to be a cap on the student numbers. This would have created a competitive market by compelling universities to vie with each other for the fixed available number of students. The report was received and acted on in 2010 by the newly elected Coalition government. Conservative members of the government would probably have allowed *no* maximum to the fee. However, a limit of £9,000 was imposed as a result of the Liberal Democrat influence within the coalition, the party having opposed tuition fees in the 2010 General Election. A strong Conservative government would have made no limit on fees in order to engender a fully-fledged competitive market. In the event, most universities charged the maximum £9,000 fee. There were two reasons for this: first they preferred the high income to sustain teaching quality, and second because most universities did not want to be seen as 'cut-price' or 'down-market' institutions which would deter student applications. Again, the notion of a market based on differential pricing collapsed. The Coalition government made some desperate efforts to encourage universities to charge lower fees by offering the recruitment of additional students in 2012 which could only be used at a £6,000 fee, but few institutions responded to this, most being further education colleges teaching HE courses.

Despite the massive rise in fees charged by all the universities, there was no reduction in the overall applications: the market for degrees was so strong, and the student loan meant that the undergraduate did not have to pay up front. While the fees and loans reduced the number of mature and part-time students, the numbers from schools kept coming in. Wolf (2002), in an international study, found that the introduction of, and increases in, student fees does not reduce the numbers in HE, nor, as in Australia where fees were removed, did it *increase* the numbers. In 2014 the cap on student numbers was lifted, meaning that universities could recruit any number of students, all paying a £9,000 fee. Frank et al. (2019) argue that this effectively abolished the market which was intended to make universities efficient. Universities were simply able to recruit lower-qualified students who were all willing to pay the fee: 'Even a completely hapless management would run a surplus in this environment' (p. 3).

The Coalition government, of course, presented the increase in fees as a fiscal measure to reduce the national financial deficit. However, as Morgan (2011) points out, the government saves little from the arrangement: it will have to find all the funding for student loans, much of which will never be repaid. Tuition fees should, then, be seen as continuing marketisation, putting the control of HE into the hands of the student 'customer'.

> **Questions for reflection**
>
> 1. Who pays for university degrees?
> 2. Some people argue that HE should be free. Others argue that graduates benefit from their degrees and should contribute to their education. What are the economic arguments for and against these positions?
> 3. The National Student Survey (2013) enables students to report on the quality of their education. What is the case for students having power over their university in this way? Can you see any problems with it?

University knowledge in the market

The discourse about tuition fees has been exclusively in terms of finance and the controversy about access to HE for the financially disadvantaged. But the increased power of the student voice through the market has forced a change in the nature of the university curriculum and in who makes decisions about it. This occurs at two levels: first is the selection of subjects included in the university with the decline of traditional subjects such as philosophy – Kant's basis of the knowledge in the modern university – and the rise of 'popular' subjects: sports science, dance, commercial music. The second is the student's choice of modules within a subject where popular and 'easy' knowledge is selected. It is reflected in the high incidence of expressed student dissatisfaction and demands for refunds. In 2017–2018 there were 1,635 complaints to the Office of the Independent Adjudicator and £650,000 paid in refunds (Adams, 2018c).

Students exercising their choice can be depicted as the 'democratisation of knowledge' (Delanty, 2001). But it raises the larger question of whether Humboldt's vision of the relationship between the state, knowledge, culture and the university should slip into the hands of a market. The commitment of successive British governments to neoliberal free-market economics as a means of managing all public services should be challenged, and universities should be leading on confronting this. While the university operates as a business in a free market with the first priority of attracting fee-paying customers, it is difficult to see an optimistic future for the university's definition of knowledge. While Kant worried that university knowledge should not be 'for the service of the state', we should now, surely, be arguing that knowledge should not simply be at the service of the market.

The effects of competition in the market

At the time of writing – June 2019 – the drive towards marketised HE in England and Wales can be seen to be nearing completion with universities operating as corporations in a business world. Energy is directed towards attracting well-qualified applicants paying their fees and marketing departments in universities are forever growing, sometimes breaking the rules of the Advertising Standards Association by making excessive claims for themselves (Sweeney and Weale, 2017). A case of exaggerated marketing was highlighted in June 2019 when an overseas student sued Anglia Ruskin University for falsely advertising that her course International Business Strategy would offer 'high-quality teaching'. She received an out-of-court settlement of £61,000.

The focus of attention is less upon academic quality and the pursuit of truth of the modern university, but the pursuit of high ratings in the NSS (2013) and in the many guide-to-university ratings in the broadsheet media. Guides such as those in the *Times* (2018) produce league tables ranking universities on a long list of criteria by subject, student satisfaction in the NSS scores, teaching resources, entry tariff and graduate employment. HE has become an evaluated commodity and, like reading the motor car ratings in *What Car Magazine*, applicants can make an informed choice for their purchase

Gray's (1998) point that free markets actually need state intervention can be seen in the government's construction of a series of measures and monitoring devices for HE: the Research Excellence Framework (REF), the Teaching Excellence Framework (TEF), the Knowledge Exchange Framework (KEF) and the Office for Students (OfS). The REF (REF2021), replacing the Research Assessment Exercise (RAE) of 2008, was originated in 2014 to monitor the quality of each university's research output on a subject by subject basis.

It was designed to inform the government on how to distribute research funding, giving the largest amount to those departments with the highest scores. The system has the effect of perpetuating quality differences in that those universities with the best research profile receive the highest funding and so continue to produce the best research. For example, in the 2014 REF 33 per cent of the total funding went to only five universities. While the REF was not designed as a marketing tool, universities are able to use their subject REF ranking to advertise their quality to applicants.

The Teaching Excellence and Student Outcomes Framework (DfE, 2018) was introduced in 2017–2018 to measure teaching quality across HE in the United Kingdom 'with a view to driving up quality, and better inform students when making applications'. Ratings (Gold, Silver, Bronze or Provisional) are awarded at provider-level, and from 2019 to 2020 they are awarded at subject-level. Data to inform the grading is drawn from the NSS; there is no observation of teaching, as in Ofsted's inspection of teaching in schools.

The KEF (Research England, 2018) is designed to 'further a culture of continuous improvement in universities by providing a package of support to keep English university knowledge exchange operating at a world class standard'. The scheme is to ensure that universities link with employers and industry to increase the vocational orientation of HE and embed it further into industry, as Barnett (2000: 20) says, 'dissolving into the wider world'.

The OfS was implemented in January 2018 with the combination of Higher Education Funding Council for England (HEFCE) and the Office for Fair Access (OfFA). OfS is a regulatory body with the stated aims that students in HE:

1. are supported to access, succeed in, and progress from, higher education;
2. receive a high-quality academic experience, and their interests are protected while they study or in the event of provider, campus or course closure;
3. are able to progress into employment or further study, and their qualifications hold their value over time;
4. receive value for money.

(OfS, 2018)

Again, it is possible to see OfS as a support for applicants and students in HE, but its underlying project is to ensure that the market 'works'. Point 4 of the aims is perhaps the most significant.

Independence

British universities are not government-owned but are independent bodies. All have charters or degree-awarding powers, and their governance, while subject to various government guidelines, is independent. The vast majority of universities in the United Kingdom are funded by the state through the student loans scheme. There are only five 'private' British universities: the University of Buckingham, Regent's University London, BPP University, Arden University and the profit-making University of Law. They are 'private' only in that their students cannot use the government loan scheme. There are several private higher education colleges, which also hold degree-awarding powers, and a number of private foreign universities have campuses located in the United Kingdom, mostly in London. It is likely that the number of private universities will increase.

It is a part of the neoliberal agenda to detach the government from the governance and management of universities. Before the introduction of full student fees in 2010 the government funded universities directly through the HEFCE. The student loan scheme is managed by the Student Loans Company (SLC), a government-owned body. Students did not have to pay fees up front: they were paid from the loan, and a means-tested loan was available to contribute to living costs. Repayment of loans began when the graduate's salary reached £21,000 and the interest charged on outstanding debt was six per cent, but the loan is written off after 30 years. (There are no university fees in Scotland and reduced fees in Northern Ireland for NI residents.)

That students in England were shouldering much of the cost of HE is self-evident. However, worries about high levels of debt were mitigated by Martin Lewis of moneysavingexpert.com who pointed out that the amount of debt to be repaid can be actually much less than the individual's total. Again, it was part of the neoliberal agenda that students should *be seen* to be paying the total cost in a HE market at no cost to the government purse. And so it appeared until 17 December 2018 when the Office for National Statistics (ONS, 2018) announced that the high proportion of unpaid student debt, estimated at £12bn per annum, should be made visible and included in the figures for government annual deficit.

As mentioned in the introduction, outrage over vice chancellors' pay came from Lord Adonis and other politicians, featuring as the VCs of Bath's two universities (Kyereme, 2017). The magnitude of VC pay, and the number of senior staff paid over £100,000 a year are a symptom of the marketised university: to attract the best the institution has to pay high salaries. Other forms of industry offer high salaries to their chief executive officers in order to attract the right quality of applicant. But this is to assume that the university is alongside industrial organisations. It appears that this must now be made, despite the protests and the implementation of a rather weak self-imposed 'code of practice' designed to assuage the anger (Adams, 2018a). Another effect of the market is the purchasing of professors with high research ranking in order to boost the university's research output and to gain government funding from the REF (Adams, 2018b).

Another point mentioned in the introduction is the wealth of the university sector, a result of successive years of income from the £9,000 plus tuition fees. HE was reported in 2016 to have an overall surplus of £1.8bn (Adams, 2016). The prosperity of the universities enabled them to become active players in the financial markets, taking on multi-million-pound loans for new buildings (International Finance Review, 2018). A characteristic of being in a market is that an institution needs to be constantly expanding.

However, with the autumn 2018 student entry universities began to feel the market's pinch. It was a simple demographic – a sharp decline in the number of 18-year-olds – that reduced the multiple of fees across the board. The market with so-called 'variable' fees had never worked to make universities compete on a financial basis because they all charged the same. Suddenly in September 2018 there were 'special offers': no reductions in fees, but applicants with good grade predictions were given unconditional offers, free iPads or cash-back remuneration for those exceeding the offer grades. Again, the clumsy marketing strategies of universities was exposed in January 2019 when the OfS threatened universities with de-registration if they put pressure on applicants by offering them unconditional places if they put the university as first choice.

University finances were further threatened with the publication of the Augar Report (HMG, 2019) on tertiary (post-18) education. In response to the intensity of political discussion of student fees Teresa May in February 2018 commissioned equites broker Philip Augar to review the funding of both further and higher education. Augur was to look at how future students would contribute to the cost of their studies, including the level, terms and duration of their contribution. The review was the first since the Robbins Report of 1963, but was restricted to the nature and means of funding. The prime minister had discounted the idea of moving back to a fully taxpayer-funded system, leaving universities in the competitive market. Further education (FE) had always been underfunded, and Augur's main recommendation was a reduction in university fees to £7,500that and that FE colleges and independent training providers (ITPs) should receive an increased share of resources with. Fees would be retitled 'the Student Contribution System'. The increase in FE should include a growth of technical qualifications suited to the needs of industry. There would be no capping of student numbers, but there should be a reduction in university courses which do not meet industry's needs and lead to disappointing career outcomes for students. Student loans would continue but the period for repayment extended from 30 to 40 years.

Augur's recommendations were criticised for being 'regressive' in that the longer repayment term meant that those on higher graduate incomes, for example those working in banking or the City, would pay off their loans quickly, whereas those on lower incomes – teachers and nurses – would pay interest for longer, effectively subsidising wealthier graduates. Augar could be said to be '*progressive*' in that it proposed a £3,000-per-year maintenance grant for students from low-income families. However, the commission was based on the continuing neoliberal assumption that HE is a commodity for be purchased and paid for by its consumer.

Conclusion

Until 2018 the university sector has continued to grow in finance and real estate. The surpluses generated by the continuing stream of student fees gave managers and governors confidence not just to build and expand, but to borrow funds to expand even further. In this respect their independence was strengthened. However, with the reduction in income in the autumn of 2018, and with the likely reduction in fees in the Augar Report, it became clear that some universities may be in financial difficulties with over-borrowing of loans they would not be able to repay. Moody's, the international credit ratings agency gave negative warnings on seven of the nine UK universities that have borrowed funds through international capital markets. Only Oxford and Cambridge with their large and ancient endowment funds were rated secure by Moody's (2019). Michael Barber, Head of the OfS, stated that the government would not bail out universities that got into debt. This was a 'purist' neoliberal stance: governments should not be bailing out failing companies. However, it was revealed that the OfS had indeed covered the £1m shortfall in one university which was not named. This was an indication that the pure neoliberal stance was not a stable one and that the government may not be able to resist bail-outs (Adams, 2018d).

It is just possible that the extreme neoliberal economic policy on HE will come to an end or be modified. At the time of writing the policy of the Labour Party is to abolish student fees; the Education Parliamentary Select Committee, which includes politicians from both sides of the house, was calling for the re-instatement of means-tested student grants. But it is *only* a possibility!

Under the Humboldt model of HE the modern university was about the development and self-realisation of the individual through academic study. Standing outside society and government, the university's role was to define knowledge and to critique government policy and actions. That university education is now available to far more people must itself be a matter for celebration. However, government attempts to bring HE *into* the neoliberal market economy have been successful. Universities now have to operate like all commercial bodies, balancing risks of income, borrowing and expenditure. As Collini (2012) suggests in the title of his book, *What Are Universities For?*, the question is being answered as the provision for skills for industry and employment. But while university fees and employment prospects dominate the discourse today, it is up to those of us in universities – students and academics – to argue for a higher order answer the question: higher education as a public good.

Summary points

The chapter has outlined the changes which have taken place in HE with the move from the 'modern' to the 'postmodern' university in the marketplace. HE continues to be in a state of rapid and perhaps irreversible change, and more is to come as the student population fluctuates and successive governments enable the influence of the market on education. The key issue are:

- the medieval university and its continuing traditions;
- academic freedom in the modern university and its definitions of knowledge and culture;
- the nature of knowledge in the postmodern university in the neoliberal marketplace;
- the loss of academic freedom and the decline of the intellectual;
- the case for the higher education as a 'public good'.

Recommended readings

Collini, S. (2012) *What Are Universities For?* London: Penguin.
Frank, J., Gower, N. and Naef, M. (2019) *English Universities in Crisis: Markets without Competition*. Bristol: Bristol University Press.
Readings, B. (1996) *The University in Ruins*. Cambridge, MA: Harvard University Press.
Society for Research in Higher Education (SRHE). Online. Available at www.srhe.ac.uk/ (Accessed 25 January 2019).
Times Higher Education (THE). Available at https://www.timeshighereducation.com/.

References

Adams, R. (2016) Tuition fees give England universities surplus worth £1.8bn. *Guardian*, 3 March 2016. Available at: www.theguardian.com/education/2016/mar/03/tuition-fees-england-universities-surplus-balance (Accessed 2 December 2018).

Adams, R. (2018a) Universities to adopt watered-down code for vice-chancellors' pay. *Guardian*, 6 June 2018. Available at: www.theguardian.com/education/2018/jun/06/universities-to-adopt-code-vice-chancellors-pay-guidelines (Accessed 2 December 2018).

Adams, R. (2018b) UK universities hiring 'superstar' professors to boost research rankings. *Guardian*, 5 October 2018. Available at: www.theguardian.com/education/2018/oct/05/uk-universities-hiring-superstar-professors-to-boost-research-ran-kings (Accessed 2 December 2018).

Adams, R. (2018c) Student complaints about UK universities growing, says watchdog. *Guardian*, 26 April 2018. Available at: www.theguardian.com/education/2018/apr/26/student-complaints-about-uk-universities-growing-says-watchdog (Accessed 5 December 2018).

Adams, R. (2018d) Government 'could bail out universities if in financial danger'. *Guardian*, 23 November 2018. Available at: www.theguardian.com/education/2018/nov/23/government-universities-oxford-cambridge-moodys (Accessed 23 November 2018).

Adams, R. and Gamper, E. (2018) University vice-chancellors are paid far more than public sector peers. *Guardian*, 11 March 2018. Available at: www.theguardian.com/education/2018/mar/11/university-vice-chancellors-are-paid-far-more-than-public-sector-peers (Accessed 19 March 2018).

Barnett, R. (2000) *Realizing the University in an Age of Supercomplexity*. Buckingham: Society for Research into Higher Education and Open University Press.

Browne, J. (2010) *Securing a Sustainable Future for Higher Education: An Independent Review of Higher Education Funding & Student Finance*. London: DfE.

Collini, S. (2012) *What Are Universities For?* London: Penguin.

Collini, S. (2018) In UK universities there is a daily erosion of integrity. *Guardian*, 24 April 2018.

Committee on Higher Education (1963) *The Robbins Report*. London: HMSO.

Delanty, G. (2001) *Challenging Knowledge: The University in the Knowledge Society*. Buckingham: HE/Open University.

Department for Education (2018) *Teaching Excellence and Student Outcomes Framework Specification*. London: DfE.

Frank, J., Gower, N. and Naef, M. (2019) *English Universities in Crisis: Markets without Competition*. Bristol: Bristol University Press.

Gray, J. (1998) *False Dawn: The Delusions of Global Capitalism*. London: Granta.

Haddad, G. (2000) University and society: responsibilities, contracts, partnerships. In G. Neave (ed.), *The Universities' Responsibilities to Society: International Perspectives*. Issues in Higher Education. Oxford: Pergamon.

Henkel, M. (1991) *Government, Evaluation and Change*. London: Jessica Kingsley.

HMG (2019) *Independent Panel Report to the Review of Post-18 Education and Funding*. London: Open Government Licence.

International Finance Review (2018) *UK Universities Turn to Private Market as Debts Rack up*. IFR, 20 October 2018. Available at: www.ifre.com/uk-universities-turn-to-private-market-as-debts-rack-up/21359758.fullarticle (Accessed 23 March 2019).

Kant, E. (1992) *The Conflict of the Faculties*. Mary J. McGregor (trans.). Lincoln and London: University of Nebraska.

Kogan, M. and Hanney, S. (2000) *Reforming Higher Education*. London: Jessica Kingsley.

Kyereme, J. (2017) As a student, I didn't go to university to pay a vice-chancellor £800,000. *New Statesman*, 8 December 2017.

Lewis, M. (2018) *Student Loans Mythbusting*. Online. Available at: www.moneysavingexpert.com/students/student-loans-tuition-fees-changes/ (Accessed 16 December 2018).

Magna Charta Universitatum (1988) Online. Available at: www.magna-charta.org/resources/files/the-magna-charta/english (Accessed 5 December 2018).

Moody's (2019) *UK Universities Face Increased Financial Pressure from Rising Staff and Pension Costs*. Online. Available at: www.moodys.com/research/Moodys-UK-universities-face-increased-financial-pressure-from-rising-staff- PBC_1169029 (Accessed 4 June 2019).

Morgan, J. (2011) UUK head: cuts reality 'rather different to the headlines'. *Times Higher Education*, 17–23 March 2011.

National Student Survey (2013). Available at: www.thestudentsurvey.com/ (Accessed 28 February 2013).

New College Oxford (2017) *Annual Report and Financial Statements Year Ended 31 July 2017*. Oxford: New College Oxford.

Newman, J.H. (1996) *The Idea of a University*, ed. Frank M. Turner. New Haven: Yale University Press.

ONS (2018) *Accounting for Student Loans*. Online. Available at: https://blog.ons.gov.uk/2018/12/17/accounting-for-student-loans-how-we-are-improving-the-recording-of-student-loans-in-government-accounts/ (Accessed 19 December 2018).

OfS (2018) *The Regulatory Framework for Higher Education in England*. Available at: www.officeforstudents.org.uk/advice-and-guidance/regulation/the-regulatory-framework-for-higher-education-in-england/ (Accessed 4 December 2018).

Readings, B. (1996) *The University in Ruins*. Cambridge, MA: Harvard University Press.

REF2021 (2018) *Research Excellence Framework*. Available at: www.ref.ac.uk/ (Accessed 4 December 2018).

Research England (2018) *Knowledge Exchange Framework*. Available at: https://re.ukri.org/knowledge-exchange/knowledge-exchange-framework/ (Accessed 4 December 2018).

Silver, H. (1990) *A Higher Education: The Council for National Academic Awards and British Higher Education 1964–8*. Lewes: Falmer Press.

Sutton Trust (2018) *Access to Advantage*. London: Sutton Trust.

Sweeney, M. and Weale, S. (2018) Six UK universities break advertising rules with pitches to students. *Guardian*, 15 November 2017.

Times (2018) *The Complete University Guide*. Available at: www.thecompleteuniversityguide.co.uk/league-tables/rankings (Accessed 4 December 2018).

Toswell, M.J. (2017) *Today's Medieval University*. Kalamazoo, MI, and Bradford: ARC Humanities Press.

Which? University (2018) *What Is the Russell Group?* Online. Available at: https://university.which.co.uk/advice/choosing-a-course/what-is-the-russell-group (Accessed 7 December 2018).

Wolf, A. (2002) *Does Education Matter? Myths about Education and Economic Growth*. London: Penguin.

9 Education as a practice of freedom
Negotiating knowledges at a Pakistani women's organisation

Areesha Banglani

Introduction

In the development discourse, education is positioned as the catch-all remedy for all issues facing society. The empowerment of women and girls, especially in the Third World, is often couched in terms of increasing access to education. However, the education referred to is often Western and Eurocentric and, in fact, maintains social hierarchies such as those of class, gender and religion rather than diminishing them. This chapter is an exploration of the Western and neoliberal biases that impact education and the development discourse, the conversation dealing with the progress of countries and societies. By looking at a grassroots women's rights organisation, the chapter will demonstrate that the Western neoliberal education is not the only way to 'freedom'.

The argument builds on an initiative originating from and embedded in the urban slum of Maripur in Karachi, Pakistan. A grassroots 'development' organisation, hereafter referred to as 'the Center', works to provide vocational skills for women so that they can provide for themselves financially. By focusing on the everyday informal interactions of the interns of the Center, who all come from the slum, I make a case for indigenous knowledges informally shared as a way of knowing and learning. The chapter is intended to counter the idea that there is a necessity to replicate the 'developed' West and its ideas and initiatives in the struggle for liberation, while at the same time addressing the entanglement with the West and Western ideas. Hence, negotiation will be a continuous and recurring theme throughout the chapter.

I will explore the idea of negotiation through the intern's conversational and experiential learning with the aim of highlighting the ways they made use of reflection to negotiate knowledges and adapt them to their own contexts. Moreover, since the work of the Center focuses on women, the questions regarding gender dynamics are deeply embedded in my questioning of the dominant Western discourse. Thus, I begin the chapter outlining the theoretical framework in which the argument and case study are grounded.

I start with the decolonial critique of the development discourse and introduce the decolonial ideas of development, starting with the works of Escobar (1992, 1995, 1997) to highlight the Eurocentric biases of the development discourse. With the help of Grosfoguel (2011), I argue that a bottom-up approach is not meant to romanticise indigenous knowledges and cultures, but is rather an attempt at creating new parameters and paradigms of change with the people rather than as opposed to them. Thereafter, I demonstrate the entanglement of the development discourse with neoliberalism and show how 'developmental issues' such as education and women's rights have been co-opted by the hegemonic discourse resulting in a drive to create workers and not thinkers. I provide an alternate approach to the dominant developmental approach to education, that is education as the practice of freedom, based in Freire's (1970) pedagogical philosophy and hooks' (1994, 2010) work: a humane and dialogical approach to education which helps bringing to the forefront grassroots initiatives and the voices of those at the margins of society. Finally, I use a case study example to propose alternative understandings and approaches to education.

The hegemony of development

Escobar (1992: 23) argues that the discourse around development is what creates the Third World. He states: '… development can be described as an apparatus (*dispositif*) that links forms of knowledge about the Third World with the deployment of forms of power and intervention, resulting in the mapping and production of Third World societies'.

This means, the 'developed' First World not only defines the parameters of development but also defines the Third World in relation to these parameters. These ideas, of development and the Third World, originate in the Western Eurocentric discourse 'with its ensemble of systems of production, power and signification' (ibid.: 22–23). As a result, the First World speaks for the Third World, resulting in what Escobar (1992, 1995) terms the 'hegemony of development'.

The hegemony of development 'establishes a discursive practice that sets the rules of the game: who can speak, from what points of view, with what authority and according to what criteria of expertise' (Escobar, 1997: 87). The Third World is created in opposition to the First World and to achieve progress, to be 'developed', the former must necessarily replicate the standards set out by the latter. Ultimately, it is the First World that speaks for the Third World and defines the Third World's 'progress'.

Missing from this discourse is the *voice* of the Third World. Development discourse involves policies, strategies and decisions made by 'experts' sitting in offices, distant, not only physically but also epistemically, from the people affected by those policies and decisions. Thus, development discourse has been critiqued time and again for silencing the subaltern voice in its arrogance of knowing best. Development experts are either those who are from the West or those who have been trained in the Western ways of knowing. For Grosfoguel (2011: 6), this also includes Third World scholars and experts who shape their understandings in line with the development discourse, as for him the social location is as important as the epistemic location:

> the fact that one is socially located in the oppressed side of power relations does not automatically mean that he/she is epistemically thinking from a subaltern epistemic location. … Subaltern epistemic perspectives are knowledge coming from below that produces a critical perspective of hegemonic knowledge in the power relations involved.

The subaltern voice, the voice of those who are the 'targets' of development policies and initiatives, is excluded from the development discourse in a white man's burden-esque approach to development. However, the burden is now carried not only by white men but also the brown men and the brown women. Grosfoguel (2011: 3), speaking in the development context, critiques post-colonial scholars, such as Spivak (1988), Said (1979) and Bhabha (1994), stating that, even though their social location is the Third World, their epistemic location is the First World, resulting in a 'Eurocentric critique of Eurocentrism'. For him, as well as other decolonial scholars, a post-colonial critique of development results, not in the 'alternatives to development' that decolonial scholars call for, but rather alternate development, working within the same parameters albeit with different strategies.

What must be kept in mind, however, is that this is not an attempt to romanticise indigenous ways of knowing. Escobar (1995: 215) states 'the Third World should in no way be seen as a reservoir of "traditions"'. Local or indigenous knowledges and ways of being are not static. Being a part of the globalised world and post-colonial nations, these entities are in a constant state of flux, interacting and entangling with the First World, and as a result there is hardly anything that can be characterised as 'purely' indigenous. Non-West, while different from the West, finds itself entangled deeply with the West. As a result, the decolonial approach does not aim to find an indigenous utopia, but rather works with the entanglements, not only to address the imperialising erasure by the West, but also to find different paradigms and spaces in which to negotiate and re-negotiate ideas and knowledges. The point is not to trace these entities to their point of origin but rather to understand the dialogues that occur, the ideas that are adapted and the traditions that are rejected. It is rather to provide a space where one 'can experiment with different ways of organising societies and economies and of dealing with the ravages of four decades of development' (Escobar, 1992: 27).

> **Question for reflection**
>
> 1. What shapes our understandings of the Third World? What role do discourses surrounding 'development' play in this?

Education, development and the neoliberal agenda

Education has been constructed as one of the main responses to progression and prosperity. However, this idea is embedded not only in the development discourse but has also been co-opted by neoliberal understandings. In this section, I will argue that the neoliberal discourse is a discourse of desire, consumption and future which results in education and the educated becoming goods available for consumption: that is, transforming the student into a consumer and worker (or labourer).

'Neoliberalism is a politically imposed discourse, which is to say that it constitutes the hegemonic discourse of western nation states' (Olssen and Peters, 2005: 314). Because neoliberalism defines the Western discourse, it also defines the development discourse which is embedded in the Western discourse. However, with its global impact, neoliberalism affects almost every nation in the world, despite its Western origins.

The question that arises is what exactly does neoliberalism entail? According to Kontopodis (2012: 3) neoliberalism is marked by two tendencies: (a) the desire to be successful and consume – not to enjoy, share or create but to *consume* things, services, even people or immaterial goods and (b) the inability to be successful and access, appropriate and consume all those things, services and goods.

Neoliberalism creates the desire to consume, implying that the answer to one's problems and happiness can be found at the back of the store in a shopping mall or behind the screen of one's computer. Neoliberalism encourages, therefore, a look to the future, a future where the desire to consume, will be fulfilled. However, the fulfilment of desire always remains in the future and, as a result, is never attained. Moreover, this neoliberal look to the future is blinding as it is 'a certain way to look to the future while not seeing anything else' (ibid.: 3). Such a look not only distracts from the realities and issues pertaining to the current present but also overlooks the past and erases historical memory.

The neoliberal discourse, one of desire, consumption and future, has co-opted the development discourse and the discourse surrounding education whereby not only education becomes a good for consumption – highly privatised institutions and education as a status symbol – but also the student becomes available for consumption. This is achieved by education becoming, not a means of learning and acquiring knowledge, but rather a way of transferring skills, a mandatory step, a rite of passage, towards finding a job. The student is a future labourer and employee:

> producing efficient job-seekers and employees becomes the main aim of educational programs for the next generation ... schools become more and more interconnected with the job market and student development is concerned in terms of vocational education, professional orientation and development of job-finding skills.
>
> (ibid.: 4–5)

The aim of education is transformed under the neoliberal agenda to create a cheap and competitive workforce, not thinkers.

Moreover, neoliberalism results in 'suppression of oppositional critical thought and much autonomous thought and education' (Kumar and Hill, 2011: 4) as critical thinking, one that ponders over inequalities and is at odds with the neoliberal agenda. Neoliberalism not only creates and sustains inequalities, but rather exists and thrives because of them. Kontopodis writes:

> The *desire to consume* as a dominating tendency, which has spread throughout the world, marks also a deeper, less apparent, *ethical-political crisis*. It marks a crisis of ethical-political principles (individualism over altruism, competition over solidarity, hostility over peace and collaboration, homogeneity over heterogeneity) that renders almost impossible any form of non-hierarchical collective organisation.
>
> (2012: 4, italics in original)

This raises the question if neoliberalism, which thrives on inequalities, can work for equality? What implications does the neoliberal approach to education have for overcoming structural inequalities such as those of gender? Baker (2010: 3) states that the 'we can be and do anything' attitude of the neoliberalism, especially prevalent in the discourse around girls' education, leads to a masking of structural inequalities. Instead the responsibility to uplift themselves falls on women and minorities, couched in terminology of choice and self-reliance. This takes the focus away from the structure of neoliberalism which is not only based in but is sustained by these very inequalities. Baker (ibid.: 13) argues that the choices women are 'empowered' to make are often limited by external influences such as 'traditionally gendered and classed parameters'. The choices, promised to women and girls for following the path of education, are not enough to address the structural discrimination they face. Women are burdened with the responsibility of undoing the structural issues within the restraints of these choices and are consequently blamed for not achieving that impossible goal.

Does the neoliberal bias in education mean that education cannot provide the solution for dismantling structural inequalities? I argue that it is possible; however, it requires a shift in the way we understand and approach education. In the following sections I provide an alternative understanding of education in order to disentangle it from its neoliberal biases and through that turn to its alternative meaning: education as the practice of freedom.

Education as the practice of freedom

bell hooks (1994: 13) argues that the role of education and of teachers is 'to share in the intellectual and spiritual growth' of students. Hence, she argues for an engaged pedagogy, a teaching practice that emphasises wellbeing and promotes a process of self-actualisation. hooks' teaching philosophy is inspired by the works of Paulo Freire. For Freire (1970: 30), liberatory education, what he terms 'pedagogy of the oppressed', is 'a pedagogy which must be forged *with*, not *for*, the oppressed (whether individuals or peoples) in the incessant struggle to regain their humanity'.

An engaged pedagogy, one that would lead to the liberation of the oppressed from the oppressor, must come from the oppressed themselves. It is through reflection on their historical and social condition that the oppressed can wage the struggle for their liberation. Otherwise, if the oppressors continue teaching them in their own ways, telling them what to think, the relationship of oppression – the master-slave narrative – continues. The oppressor, of course, does not want the oppressed to think for themselves, as

> the oppressor knows full well that this intervention would not be to his interest. What *is* to his interest is for the people to continue in a state of submersion, impotent in the face of the oppressive reality.
>
> (ibid.: 34, italics in original)

One way in which the oppressor maintains the impotence of the oppressed in the face of oppression is through what Freire (1970: 71) terms 'the banking system of education' whereby knowledge is bestowed upon the student. The banking system of education is a top-down approach to education: the teacher knows best and will teach the students what they need to know; the role of the students is merely to be passive recipients to education, resulting in passivity of the oppressed. The banking system of education ensures that the students are integrated to the ways of knowing, seeing and being of the oppressors. Speaking in the context of Iran, Rahnema (1997: 158) states, 'literacy campaigns often turned out to be campaigns against the non-literate, rather than helping the oral populations to educate themselves and learn as they had always done'. Such an approach to education for Freire (1970: 55) 'will never propose to students that they critically consider reality'.

The neoliberal education system, as I outlined in the previous sections, could be seen as a banking system of education. It fails to provide the room for critical thinking which would challenge and question the system but instead turns the students into passive recipients of information and skills needed to support and perpetuate the dominant system. It defines not only the types of education provided but, more importantly, what education means.

To counter the banking system of education, Freire proposes education as liberation and liberation as praxis, that is, 'the action and reflection of men and women upon their world in order to transform it' (ibid.: 60). Such pedagogical philosophy and practice break away from the student-teacher relationship of giver and receiver of knowledge, but instead brings them into mutual dialogue whereby both learn from one another and, through their relations with the world in 'acts of cognition, not transferals of information' (ibid.: 64).

The role of the teacher is not to teach but to enter into a dialogue which encourages critical thinking. If one was to approach the oppressed, the 'illiterate' and which education to consume, not only will that be an imposition of the oppressor's knowledge on the oppressed but also a cultural invasion which devalues and defoliates the knowledge held by the oppressed. Such a pedagogy is only possible by working, not *for* or *on* the people, but *with* the people.

Applying his pedagogical philosophy in the context of Brazil, Freire states that for one to learn responsibility, democracy and freedom was through the *experience* of responsibility, democracy and freedom as 'that knowledge, above all others, can only be assimilated experientially' (Freire, 1973: 32). Hence, the role of the educator is to enter into dialogue, taking up the role of the students themselves, and for the students to take up the role of the teacher as well. Both not only learn from engaging with one another but also from their experience of the theoretical concepts they are discussing. Unlike the top-down approach of neoliberal systems of education, education as praxis – engaged pedagogy – is one that democratises the teaching and learning experience. This starts with the acknowledgement that the students – the oppressed, the illiterate – hold knowledges which must not only be taken into account, but also considered relevant and valuable.

Questions for reflection

1. Think about your formal schooling years, do you remember practices that might be considered liberatory?
2. What was the value placed on critical thinking, especially in terms of challenging the dominant discourses regarding gender, class, race and religion?

Engaged pedagogy in action

In this section, I put forward an alternative approach to education, one that breaks away from the neoliberal understanding and system of education. I present a case study drawing on personal research conducted in a centre providing vocational skills for women so that they can provide for themselves financially. I thereby focus on the moments of learning that happened through dialogue. However, before outlining my findings I would like to highlight that I am not arguing for the Center as a decolonial utopia, the Center's aims and practices are part of the hegemonic development discourse. Despite this, the Center provides the site for challenging such a discourse. The grassroots nature of the organisation ensures that the initiative is socially and epistemically located within the culture it wishes to impact. This means, it was initiated from the community and is being carried out with the community as opposed to being bestowed on the community. This ensures that the voice of the people being impacted by the initiative define the initiative which, in turn, enables an alternative – more liberatory – view on education.

Generally, a grassroots approach points to a movement that start at the roots of a problem or issue and develops solutions together with the affected parties. It uses collective, local action and thus brings to the forefront the voice of the subaltern, the 'targets' of development policies; it is a voice that is often missing from the dominant development discourse where experts know best. However, an entanglement with the development discourse is not always possible. Especially political parties and interests often steer such movements in directions that are more in line with neoliberal agendas and desires than those of the community. However, such forces do not necessarily exclude the potential for decolonial practices. As stated above, negotiation and contradiction are a major theme with which the decolonial method works, and it is precisely these moments of negotiation in the dominant discourse that provide us the promise for alternatives.

Moreover, because the Center works dominantly with women, it provides a perfect opportunity to reflect not only on the different power dynamics, including gender, but also on the way those dynamics are challenged through an engaged pedagogy. The Center provided the opportunity for its interns, mostly women, to learn and challenge the understandings they entered the space with. For most of the women, the Center was the only time they had the opportunity to engage with the world outside of their domestic sphere. Due to cultural and social constraints, most of these women had little or no formal schooling background.

One of the interns, Kainat, shared that she did not pursue getting a formal education as she believed she did not have the aptitude for learning or 'doing anything'. She shared that she had no confidence in herself, so much so that before coming to the Center, even during her last job at the school, she could not talk or interact with anyone, especially men, as she got anxious:

> The supervisor used to ask us questions and for our feedback but I didn't say anything. I told her that if you want to ask me something, ask me separately, not in front of the boys. I used to get confused that if I said something wrong they would laugh at me.
> (Interview, 22 February 2017)

Her reference to being uncomfortable, especially in front of the boys, highlights not only gender segregation but also the gendered hierarchies in societies whereby Kainat, without even knowing or interacting with these boys, felt her intelligence and abilities inferior to theirs. However, during her time at the Center, Ahmed, helped her change her perception and work on her self-esteem:

> He told me you have confidence inside of you, bring it out. … I always said no, I would start crying. Whenever they said anything to me, I would start crying. He said you have the strength and now I tell him that it is because of you that I am where I am now … had you not said it to me, believed in me, I would have always believed that I have no strength or talent. … Now [the director] complains why do you scream so much and I tell her that I've learnt it here at your center.
> (Interview, 22 February 2017)

Ahmed was able to help Kainat, not because of his superior intelligence as a man, but rather because that interaction provided Kainat with the opportunity to interact with that which she was uncomfortable and intimidated by. By entering into dialogue with her, Ahmed provided her with the tools she needed to question her beliefs and to reflect on broader social issues. In this instance, Ahmed took the role of the educator Freire (1973: 45) outlines whereby 'the educator's role is fundamentally to enter into dialogue with the illiterate about concrete situations'. Kainat was in a situation she was not comfortable with, and through that uncomfortable experience, with Ahmad's help, she

Education as a practice of freedom 111

learnt to be a lot more comfortable. In other words, by interacting with a world unknown to her, she made sense of the world and her relationship with it. This could be seen as empowering practice, a first step towards a more self-defined future.

Raheela's experience at the Center was similarly transformative. Raheela did not pursue secondary education as she was married young and had children early in her life. She had limited interaction with the world outside her domestic sphere. After her divorce Raheela interned at the Center due to financial reasons. Her close friend, Jennifer, stated that when Raheela first came to the Center she would not talk to anyone and she has seen that change drastically in terms of how she interacts and conducts herself. Like Kainat, Raheela was in a world she knew nothing about and found herself lost; only by interacting with it, did she learn not only about the world but also about herself. The confidence and people's skills the interns gained at the Center, allowed them to then challenge wider cultural assumptions and understandings, for example those regarding gender and religion. Kamran shared that, along with the confidence he gained while conducting outreach tasks for the Center, his perception regarding women changed as well:

> We used to think that women are less than us, that women can't do anything but after coming here I learnt that women can do a lot more than men, they can do anything ... [these ideas] I learnt from the neighborhood, the society ... before when I would take my family members somewhere, like when they would say take us out for ice-cream, I would say first wear your burqa. They would say we would be sitting in the car, you would go get the ice-cream so why should we wear a burqa but I would say no, you have to wear the burqa but last night they said you have the car tonight so take us for ice-cream again ... so I said yes let's go. They said wait let us wear the burqa first and I said no its fine come without one, I took the car and took them, I told them not to wear a burqa.
>
> (Interview, 22 March 2017)

Kamran, a teenager, had joined the internship at the Center because he was bored at home with nothing to do, and this seemed like a good opportunity to do something and gain some work experience and, as a result, learning through this experience. His learning did not come about as a result of formalised education; that was restricted to learning only the subjects that they will be tested during exams: that is, the information transfer of the banking system of education. One can even argue that the all-boys school Kamran attended perpetuated rather than challenged the gendered power dynamics in the community. Instead, through his experience at the Center and his reflection on that experience, he came to understand, negotiate and re-negotiate with ideas of gender prevalent in the Maripur community. In the words of Freire (1970: 48), 'reflection – "only true reflection" – leads to action'.

Similar to Kamran's learning experience was Nighat's anecdote regarding religion. Maripur is a religiously diverse community. However, the diversity did not necessarily result in acceptance and celebration of differences. Hindus are considered not only *kaafirs*, non-believers, but also enemies of Muslims as a result of the India-Pakistan partition. Orthodox Muslims do not share food or even water with non-believers, especially Hindus. Speaking about this, Nighat shared:

> This Center creates connections between different religions and ethnicities. I don't discriminate when it comes to sharing food and most of the girls here don't either. Everyone has their own

reasons for not sharing. Most people believe it's unhygienic and that they [Hindus] use cow's urine in their cooking as well. I used to believe that but then I saw that my Hindu friends' homes were even cleaner than ours, that idea was challenged. They use the cow's urine for prayer but I don't think they use it in their food. You can't force someone to share but I don't believe in those differences.

(Personal communication, 8 March 2017)

Nighat's story highlights the prevalence of stereotypes regarding different communities that exist not only in Maripur but in Pakistan as well. Her experience also shows that it is by interacting with such communities, by building connections and entering in dialogue with them, these stereotypes can be dispelled and the dominant understandings challenged.

The Center is a space for the community, especially women, to come together and interact with each other and the outside world. Outside of the Center, the women and young people have little opportunity to leave the domestic space in order to engage and dialogue with those different from them in terms of religion, gender, and ethnicity. By providing this opportunity, the Center creates the space for learning through experience and dialogue. The interns know one another and learn from each other, which results not only in the sharing of knowledges but also of challenging understandings and the creation of new ways of knowing. Hence, via these interactions, the women and men, partake in engaged pedagogy: they learn from one another, co-create knowledges, challenge certain conventions and reflect on social, cultural and historical conditions.

> **Question for reflection**
>
> 1. The Center, although embedded in the hegemonic development discourse, provides a viable site for alternate ideas of education. Can you think of other sites which provide the possibilities of negotiation of dominant understandings?

Conclusion

I started this chapter with a critique of the idea common in the development discourse that education is the route to freedom, especially in the Third World context. The critique is based on questioning the concept of education itself. For Freire (1970: 71), education suffers from 'narration sickness', whereby students are taught skills and information necessary to succeed professionally – and financially. What is missing from such an education is a reflection of the biases that are upheld and further perpetuated by such information transfers. The banking system of education, which I have equated to the neoliberal education system, does not address social inequalities plaguing society. Instead it pretends either that these inequalities do not exist or that such equalities would be addressed if everyone engaged in cash-yielding activities to achieve greater financial independence. Such claims by the banking system of education are neither accidental nor a result of ignorance, but rather are made to serve its purpose and aims, that is, Eurocentricism and neoliberalism. What is needed is a challenging of these hegemonic ideas and my research has attempted to bring forth one such initiative that carries the potential to do so.

My aim at the Center was to learn not only the knowledges the people of Maripur hold, but also how they negotiate with these knowledges, challenge cultural assumptions and create new norms in the process. It was about looking at negotiations and tensions that occurred within the space of the Center with indigenous ways of being and external influences. It must be kept in mind that the indigenous way of being is not one that has preserved itself historically but rather one that is constantly changing as it interacts with the world around it, and it was this interaction that I wished to learn from. Hence, this research was, at its base, about negotiations that these people make in their interaction with the world.

Dialogue and experience served as an opportunity to reflect and reason with ideas and practices different from the ones the interns held, and resulted in negotiations and the challenging of beliefs about inequalities, gender, religion and ethnicity, as well as translating into action regarding these inequalities. I interpreted this in line with Freire's pedagogical philosophy whereby reflection, dialogue and a humanising pedagogy result in action.

The case study highlighted a different possibility in approaching 'development issues'. Instead of calling to experts to help guide those in marginal and subaltern positions, I argue for treating the indigenous populations as experts. By trusting their ability to reflect, understand and negotiate, not only their conditions, but also of those around them with whom they interact, we can potentially dismantle the power differentials between different groups and work towards an equal future. Acknowledging and valuing the power of local dialogue as well as the knowledges held by indigenous groups can lead to the possibility of not only learning without imposed imperial ideas but more importantly, undoing and unpacking those ideas.

Summary points

- In the hegemonic development discourse, education is positioned as the solution to all of society's ills. However, such an education is Western and Eurocentric, devalues indigenous knowledges and is embedded in the neoliberal discourse.
- As a result, education has become a sort of information and skills transfer aimed at turning students into labour and employee as opposed to critical thinkers.
- For education to be the practice of freedom, it must challenge and question the structures of power. One way to achieve this is through an 'engaged pedagogical approach' whereby the students and teachers enter into a dialogue and learn from each other's experience.
- According to an engaged pedagogy, everyone carries with themselves valuable knowledges and experiences that others can learn from. The role of an education is not to replace these knowledges but rather work with them to create new ones.
- An engaged pedagogy allows the opportunity to understand, reflect, and negotiate with ideas to apply them critically in our understanding of the world. Such an approach avoids the imposition of ideas instead allows everyone the opportunity to contribute and author in line with their experiences.
- The possibility of engaging in such decolonial practices is not through getting rid of the Western influences but rather in the moments of negotiation that present themselves as a consequence of deep entanglement of Western and indigenous worlds and ideas.

Recommended readings

Freire, P. (1998). *Pedagogy of Freedom: Ethics, Democracy and Civic Courage*. Lanham, MD: Rowman & Littlefield.
Freire, P. and Freire, A.M.A. (1994) *Pedagogy of Hope: Reliving Pedagogy of the Oppressed*. New York: Continuum.
hooks, b. (2003). *Teaching Community: A Pedagogy of Hope*. New York: Routledge.
Roy, S. (2015) The Indian women's movement: within and beyond NGOisation. *Journal of South Asian Development*, 10(1), pp. 96–117.

References

Baker, A.C., Jensen, P.J. and Kolb, D.A. (2005) Conversation as experiential learning. *Management Learning*, 36(4), pp. 411–427.
Bhabha, H.K. (1994) *The Location of Culture*. London: Routledge.
Escobar, A. (1992) Imagining a post-development era? Critical thought, development and social movements. *Social Text*, 31/32, pp. 20–56.
Escobar, A. (1995) Imagining a post-development era. In J. Crush (ed.), *Power of Development*. Abingdon: Routledge.
Escobar, A. (1997) The making and unmaking of the third world through development. In M. Rahnema and V. Bawtree (eds.), *The Post Development Reader*. London: Zed Books.
Freire, P. (1970) *Pedagogy of the Oppressed*. London: Penguin Books.
Freire, P. (1973) *Education for Critical Consciousness*. New York: Seabury Press.
Grosfoguel, R. (2011) Decolonising post-colonial studies and paradigms of political economy: transmodernity, decolonial thinking, and global coloniality. *Transmodernity: Journal of Peripheral Cultural Production of the Luso Hispanic World*, 1(1). Available at: http://dialogoglobal.com/texts/grosfoguel/Grosfoguel-Decolonizing-Pol-Econ-and-Postcolonial.pdf (Accessed 3 October 2019).
hooks, b. (1994) *Teaching to Transgress: Education as the Practice of Freedom*. New York: Routledge.
hooks, b. (2010) *Teaching Critical Thinking: Practical Wisdom*. Abingdon: Routledge.
Kontopodis, M. (2012) *Neoliberalism, Pedagogy and Human Development: Exploring Time, Mediation, and Collectivity in Contemporary Schools* (Vol. 77). Abingdon: Routledge.
Kumar, R. and Hill, D. (2011) Neoliberal capitalism and education: Introduction. In R. Kumar and D. Hill (eds.), *Global Neoliberalism and Education and Its Consequences*. New York: Routledge.
Olssen, M. and Peters, M.A. (2005) Neoliberalism, higher education and the knowledge economy: from the free market to knowledge capitalism. *Journal of Education Policy*, 20(3), pp. 313–345.
Rahnema, M. (1997) Towards post-development: searching for signposts, a new language and new paradigms. In M. Rahnema and V. Bawtree (eds.), *The Post Development Reader*. London: Zed Books.
Said, E.W. (1979) *Orientalism*. Vintage.
Spivak, G.C. (1988) Can the subaltern speak? In R. Morris (ed.), *Can the Subaltern Speak? Reflections on the History of an Idea*. New York: Columbia University Press.

10 Concluding remarks on the importance of criticality in uncertain times

Jessie A. Bustillos Morales and Sandra Abegglen

Reflecting on expectations

We hope that whatever you have read in this book has helped you to think through education, both as what happens in school and as a wider discussion that touches all parts of society. You might agree or disagree with some of the arguments put forward in the book. You may still want to research and find more about some of the topics explored. If you feel a little confused or sceptical you are on the verge of discovering more and thinking further about education and society overall. We strongly suggest you continue to explore, question and formulate your own views by engaging with literature, research and, of course, parts of your experience. The book was written to stretch your educational imagination and to help you become more critical about the topic.

> **Question for reflection**
>
> 1. Consider reviewing chapters together with others and compile a short summary of each work. You may also want to share lists of relevant books with others to further expand your understanding.

One of the main ways in which we have tried to encourage you to think about education more openly, is to present chapters with different frameworks. Engaging you with classical theory, more recent terms and notions, and insightful arguments, we hope you have a firmer grasp of the basic idea underlying all chapters: how economics co-opts the world of education. Analysing the social world is not easy because we are immersed in it all the time; it's like when people say, 'fish don't know they're in water'; we cannot always see the social world because it is so familiar. Education is a very mundane part of our social lives, but throughout this book, we have tried to make you pause and doubt the reasons why you think we do the things we do.

> **Question for reflection**
>
> 1. Why not draft a list of common 'background' themes and issues that you have detected in the book? You could also put together a collage or piece of art that reflects what you have learned – and which you can expand as you continue learning about the topic.

From the outset, we have suggested that much of our thinking around education is shaped by what we are told education is. Throughout our lives, our teachers, our parents, our peers, have told us what education is for. Nevertheless, this is not the whole story, governments dictate what happens in educational institutions through social and educational policy. Moreover, education has become a fixed aspect of political agendas around the world; there are hardly any political speeches that do not include political statements on education. When education is talked about by governments, it is often as an instrument to either secure economic balance, or enable economic prosperity. This book has sought to problematise these emerging affiliations between education and the economy.

> **Question for reflection**
>
> 1. What are political leaders in your country saying about education? Follow the news media over the next couple of weeks and make notes of particular statements and standpoints. Consider what this all means for education: What sort of image is conveyed?

The apparent complexity of economics creates a form of distance from the public understanding. This book aimed to explain in simple terms and examples how economics works, whilst also harnessing educational implications. We hope that the topics developed have engaged you critically and have nudged you towards exploring further. From thinking about why we have an education system in the first place to thinking about how the established educational system helps reproduce the economic conditions that form our experience. Making sense of it all is a huge task, and this book tried to strike the right balance between two challenges, the illusive unwillingness we all have to understand economics, and the difficulty of being critical about something so customary as education.

With regard to education, whatever stance we support or critique, it is imperative that we do not feel too comfortable, or readily accept a set of views. Instead, if we are to remain engaged critically, a more unbiased approach might help us see the effects of any proposed change, or ideology. Also, once we adhere to a doctrine and advocate it unproblematically, we are potentially putting some values and groups of people in a disadvantageous position. By accepting an ideology or view decidedly we cease to be critical. We hope that in reading this book you can develop a sensitivity and ambivalence which fosters your criticality about the subject. We believe that when you doubt and hesitate, you are taking a step forward towards critical thinking.

Towards uncertain educational futures

The future of education will be tested by technological advances, by environmental crises, but very importantly, by further pressures from economic contexts. Education is always undergoing a crisis of some sort. Philosopher Hanna Arendt (1954) suggests two key reasons for this in her essay *The Crisis in Education*. Firstly, we fail education in trying to instruct young minds with the ways of the past. Arendt argues:

> But even the children one wishes to educate to be citizens of a utopian morrow are actually denied their own future role in the body politic, for, from the standpoint of the new ones, whatever new the adult world may propose is necessarily older than they themselves. It is in the

very nature of the human condition that each new generation grows into an old world, so that to prepare a new generation for a new world can only mean that one wishes to strike from the newcomers' hands their own chance at the new.

(1954: 3)

Secondly, Arendt contends that politics corrupts and undermines the potential education has. In her view education can easily become a political weapon, a weapon which has historically been used to debase criticality, freedom and democracy. Arendt reflects further:

in Europe, the belief that one must begin with the children if one wishes to produce new conditions has remained principally the monopoly of revolutionary movements of tyrannical cast which, when they came to power, took the children away from their parents and simply indoctrinated them.

(1954: 3)

These arguments resonate with Arendt's experience since she and her mother fled Nazi Germany in 1933. Arendt remarks: 'Education can play no part in politics ... the word "education" has an evil sound in politics; there is a pretense of education, when the real purpose is coercion without the use of force' (1954: 3).

As we can see, Arendt was highly distrustful of political involvement in education; in her view, politics perverts education. Knowledge becomes doctrine, students are pacified and learning becomes merely a means to an end, in Arendt's view, a political end. In Arendt's philosophy education should remain untouched by the pervasive world of politics. Arendt outlines many issues that are easily overlooked. One of the issues highlighted is how within politics education is turned to very specific objectives. Whether they are the indoctrination into political rhetoric or the reproduction of particular skills, education is curtailed and contained. Another important issue is that of the reduction of learning to an empty, predictable process. Arendt contends:

one cannot educate without at the same time teaching; an education without learning is empty and therefore degenerates with great ease into moral emotional rhetoric. But one can quite easily teach without educating, and one can go on learning to the end of one's days without for that reason becoming educated.

(1954: 13)

Yet, Arendt's essay also offers hope. While she states that education is in a state of crisis, she also says,

a crisis becomes a disaster only when we respond to it with preformed judgments, that is, with prejudices. Such an attitude not only sharpens the crisis but makes us forfeit the experience of reality and the opportunity for reflection it provides.

(Arendt, 1954: 1)

Arendt invites us to reflect further, to not pass on the opportunity to think critically, to engage in thinking as an activity, and not just because we have a qualification to attain.

Throughout this book the pervasiveness of economics has been seen as a threat to some of the educational values described by Arendt. Education has had to face up to privatisation, commodification, competition and more public scrutiny as to how it contributes value to the economic reality. Giroux (2014: 1) labels our current economic times as 'economic Darwinism', marked by the logic of the survival of the fittest, and that political agendas are offering up public education on a plate to these economic forces. The future of education hangs in a delicate balance between its duty to people, and its duty to the State.

Both theorists, Arendt and Giroux, although writing in different times, see the attack on education by politics and economics, as an attack on the future of democracy, public good and justice. To this effect, Giroux and Arendt are both very concerned with the notion of criticality. Whilst Arendt writes to warn of the effects of political' involvement in education, Giroux (2014: 2) strongly rejects both politics and economics, stating, 'another characteristic of this crushing form of economic Darwinism is that it thrives in a kind of social amnesia, that erases critical thought, historical analysis, and any understanding of broader systemic relations'.

The importance of criticality cannot be underestimated, as it might just be the thing that balances out the changes and uncertain climate in which education happens. For now, at the close of this book, we can take some time and speculate about the future. As we have explored the issues threatening education and public engagement with criticality, we can appreciate they have a long-running history with complex effects. Despite our efforts a solution will always seem out of our reach. Yet, and perhaps more importantly, a critical appreciation of the continued effects that different forces, whether economic or political, have on education is the highest position we can aspire to. Perhaps this discerning and inquisitive attitude towards the world as a whole is what it means to be truly educated.

References

Arendt, H. (1954) *The Crisis in Education*. Available at: https://thi.ucsc.edu/wp-content/uploads/2016/09/Arendt-Crisis_In_Education-1954.pdf (Accessed 12 September 2019).

Giroux, H. (2014) *Neoliberalism's War on Higher Education*. Chicago: Haymarket Books.

Index

Abegglen, S. 5, 6
Academies Act 54
academy(ies) 42, 54, 58–60
Adams, J. 55
Adams, R. 90, 97, 99, 101
agency 23, 32, 40–41, 61, 78
Aitken, S. 32
Allen, G. 51
Allen, R. 55
Althusser, L. 4, 53, 67, 78–79, 82–83, 88
analyses: economic analyses 13, 68, 75
Angner, E. 13–14
Anthropocene 23, 33–34
Apple, M. 59
Archer, L. 57
Arendt, H. 6–7, 116–118
Aronowitz, S. 86
Arrow, K.J. 66
austerity 5, 90
authoritarianism 38–39, 47–48, 59
authority 34, 37–48, 61, 82–83, 88, 91, 93–94, 105
autonomy 38, 54–56, 92

Baker, A.C. 107
Ball, S. 49–54, 60, 88
bank(s) 16, 71, 90
banking crisis, 2008 90
Baptiste, I. 75
Barnett, R. 98
Bartlett, S. 4
Bauman, Z. 41
Beck, U. 41
Becker, G.S. 65–66
Beckett, K.S. 4
behaviour: economic behaviour 13–17
behavioural economics 7, 14–17
Benasayag, M. 41, 44–45, 47
Bhabha, H.K. 106
bias: cognitive bias 14; neoliberal bias 104–108; university bias 96

Biesta, G.J.J. 7, 43, 49
Bilington, R. 69
Bingham, C. 38
Blair, M. 15
Blair, T. 7
Blanden, J. 85
Blaug, M. 66–67
Blundell, D. 24, 26, 33
Bologna: Bologna Declaration 93; Bologna Process 92–93; University of Bologna 92
Bolton, S. 80
Bonneuil, C. 33
Boumans, M. 17
Bowles, S. 67–68
boys: education of boys 80; employment of boys 27–29
Bradbury, A. 57
Briggs, A. 24–25, 54
Britain 25–29, 50, 81, 93
Brock-Utne, B. 9
Brown, W. 68
Browne, J. 96
budget 27, 90
Bugra, A. 69–70
Burgess, S. 56
business 42, 52–58, 87, 90–98
Bustillos Morales, J.A. 5–6

Cain, G.G. 67
Cambridge 101
Camerer, C. 13–14
capitalism 15, 31, 38, 41, 95
Caraway, T.L. 80
career(s) 51, 57, 59, 67, 77, 80, 82, 85, 88, 100
Carr, D. 2
Cartwright, E. 12–14
case study 44, 104–109
Catholics 24
Chang, H. 20
childhood 8, 23–34

choice: choice and economics 12–14; choice and education 70–73; choice and inequalities 80; choice and neoliberalism 50–61; parental choice 54–56
Church of England 24
citizenship 26
Clandinin, D.J. 43
class: middle-class 25, 50, 56–58, 60–61, 77, 81, 87, 96; social class(es) 51, 56, 67, 77–79, 81–82; working-class 25, 29, 50, 53, 55–57, 59–61, 77, 81, 87, 95
climate change 23, 33–35
Colander, D. 13, 16
colleges 6, 87, 91, 93–94, 96, 99–100
Collini, S. 93, 101
Committee on Higher Education (Robbins) 93, 100
community(ies) 2, 7, 37, 41, 54–55, 60, 77–78, 109–112
company(ies) 6, 67–68, 70, 72–74, 79–80, 87, 101
competition: competition and economics 14–15; competition and education 1–5, 8, 37, 50–56, 77; competition and human capital 64–67, 70–71; competition and inequalities 77, 85; competition and trust 37, 44–48; competition and universities 96–98; market competition 15, 50, 96
consumption 12, 65–66, 106–107
Contreras, D.J. 43
Cosentino, V. 41, 43
cost 3, 5–6, 13, 64–66, 69–70, 73, 82, 85, 96, 99–100
crisis: banking crisis 90; crisis of authority 40–44; ecological crisis 33; economic crisis 16; educational crisis and Arendt 116–117
Crook, D. xii
culture: national culture 92; performativity culture 52–53, 57, 60–61; school culture 43
Cunningham, H. 28–29
curriculum: curriculum and education 53–55; curriculum and human capital theory 70; curriculum metrics 83–87; curriculum and the university 94–97; hidden curriculum 57
customers: students as customers 6, 42, 97

De Graaf, F. 16
De Muijnck, S. 16
Delanty, G. 97
democracy 86, 109
Denison, E. 65–66
Department for Education 17
deprivation 78
Dewey, J. 1
Department for Education (DfE) 56–57, 60, 98
Department for Education and Skills (DfES) 51
digital revolution 81
Diotima 37–39
Diptee, A.A. 28

discourse: economic-driven discourse 5–9, 37; educational discourse 50, 56–58, 60; development discourse 104–110; human capital theory and discourse 74; neoliberal discourse 83, 86; pedagogical discourse 42; university and discourse 97, 101
discrimination 15, 80–81, 107
diversity 42, 111
Dufour, B. 4
Dukes, P. 33

Earle, J. 19, 33
early years 51, 57, 59
EBacc 55
economy: knowledge economy 6, 52, 55, 71–74
economics: behavioural economics 14; feminist economics 15, 18; macroeconomics 13; microeconomics 12; neoclassical economics 13–14, 16, 18–20
Eden, C. 80
education: education system 38, 44, 50, 53, 61, 77–78, 82–83, 86–87, 108, 112, 116; elementary education 23, 26, 30; higher education 6, 9, 29, 57, 61, 70, 78, 85–87, 90–98; primary education 30; secondary education 12–13, 16–17, 19, 26, 51, 84, 111
educational institutions 2–3, 5–6, 42, 70, 116
educational policy 8, 42, 51–54, 60, 116
education studies 4, 10
edu-factory 77, 86
effectiveness: cost-effectiveness 6; school effectiveness 52
Elementary Education Act 23–24, 26, 29
elite: intellectual elite 90, 95; privileged elite, 77, 82–84, 88
employment: children's employment 27–29; curricula and employment 39; human capital theory and employment 67, 69–72; precarious employment 78–81, 84–86
Engelhardt, L. 14
England 8, 23–24, 90, 93, 97, 99
Enlightenment 32, 35, 91
entrepreneurial: entrepreneurial economics 68; entrepreneurial education 70; entrepreneurial employment 79–80; entrepreneurial mindset 58; entrepreneurial self 58
epistemic 105, 109
equality: equality of opportunity 91
Escobar, A. 104–106
ethnicity 15, 32, 78, 112–113
eurocentric 104–105, 112
Europe(ean) 16, 32–33, 42, 90–93
everyday life 2, 14, 40–44
exploitation: exploitation and Althusser 84; exploitation and the free-market 80

Fauser, H. 18
Feminism 37–38, 41, 43
First World War 27
Fischer, L. 20
Foucault, M. 5, 8, 16, 52–53, 58–59, 68
France 18, 93
Frank, J. 96
Frank, R. 16
Fredrickson, C. 81
free schools 54–55
Freire, P. 105, 108–110, 113–114
Friedman, M. 77

Gash, V. 84–85
Gatto, J. 59
GCSEs 55
gender: gender and childhood 32; gender dynamics 104; gender pay gap 80–81; gender and power 110–111; gender relations 15
Germany 17–18, 26, 88, 93, 117
Gerrard, J. 51, 54
Giddens, A. 41, 49
gig economy 77–81
Gilead, T. 75
Gillies, D. 74
Giroux, H. 6–7, 78, 86–87, 118
globalisation 41, 71
Gorz, A. 69
graduate(s) 67, 93, 98–100
Graham, L. 59
grassroots 104–105, 109
Gray, J. 96, 98
Greevy, H. 55
Grol, R. 13, 17
Grosfoguel, R. 104–105
gross national product (GNP) 66
growth: economic growth 13, 30, 64–66, 70, 73, 77–78

Haddad, G. 92
Hall, S. 5
Hansard, H.C. 24–25
hardship 5, 78
Harvard Political Review 10
Hayekian 50
hegemonic: hegemonic culture 44; hegemonic discourse 105–106; hegemonic knowledge 105; hegemonic relations 69
Hendrick, H. 26–27, 35
Henkel, M. 94
Her Majesty's Government (HMG) 100
Heukelom, F. 13–14
Higham, R. 55
higher education: higher education and the edu-factory 86–87; higher education in Europe 92–93; higher education and fees 96; higher education and knowledge 97; higher education and the neoliberal subject 57; higher education and the precariat 77, 85; higher education system 6, 86
Higher Education Funding Council for England (HEFCE) 98–99
Holocene 23
homo economicus 68
hooks, b. 108, 114
Horn, P. 24–29
House of Commons 23
human: human (economic) behaviour 7, 12–13, 17, 68; human capital 8, 10, 15, 30, 32, 34, 42; human rights 30
human capital theory (HCT) 30, 64–68, 70, 72, 74
Humboldt, W. 91–92, 94–95, 97, 101

ideology: dominant ideology 4, 53, 57; ideology of utility 37; neoliberal ideology 39, 41, 44, 47, 53
income: family income 24–25, 27, 29; income distribution 65; income and wages 14; national income 66
indigenous 104, 106, 113
individualism 38, 48, 107
industrial revolution 27, 91
inequality 8, 15–16, 78, 80
insecurity 58, 77, 81, 88
International Finance Review 100
Italy 41–43, 93

James, A. 32

Kahneman, D. 14
Kalleberg, A. 84
Kant, E. 92, 97
Kessler, S. 88
Keynesian 50, 71, 81, 90, 92
Kiel, M. 6
Kilpi-Jakonen, E. 85
Kjørholt, A.T. 30
knowledge economy 6, 52, 55, 71–74
Knowledge Excellence Framework (KEF) 98
Kogan, M. 94
Kontopodis, M. 107
Kumar, R.107
Kyereme, J. 99

labour: child labour 23–24, 26–27, 30; manual labour 29
Lascioli, A. 42
Lauder, H. 71
league table(s) 1, 6, 31, 85, 87, 98
Levitas, R. 83
Lewis, M. 99
Lewis, S.L. 33, 35
literacy: economic literacy 17
loans: student loans 86, 97, 99–100
local education authority (LEA) 54, 93

Magna Charta Universitatum 92
Maguire, M. 57
Mäki, U. 17
Mankiw, N. 13, 19
market: education market 99; employment market 8, 37, 39, 67; job market 51, 81
Marshall, A. 65
Marshall, J. 4
Marx, K. 78, 84, 88
McDonough, B. 80–81, 83
McGimpsey, I. 50, 53, 58
McMullin, P. 85
Mecenero, M.C. 41, 43
Mincer, J. 65
Ministry of National Education (MoNE) 71
minority(ies) 29, 55, 57, 107
Mitchell, G. 60
Moody's 100
Morgan, J. 97
Morgan, M. 13, 17
Morrin, K. 58
Mortimore, P. 52
Morton, T. 33, 35
Muller, J. 87
Muraro, L. 26, 38–40, 47
Mutaner, C. 79

National Student Survey (NSS) 97
Neilson, D. 18
neoclassical: neoclassical economics 7, 13–14, 16, 18–20; neoclassical theory 19
neoliberal: neoliberal bias 104–108; neoliberal discourse 83, 86; neoliberal ideology 39, 41, 44, 47, 53; neoliberal politics 50
neoliberalism 37–39, 41, 43, 47–48, 68
New College Oxford 91
Newman, J.H. 92
North America 42
Nussbaum, M. 42

Organisation for European Economic Co-operation and Development (OECD) 64, 70–71, 75, 84
Office for Students (OfS) 98–101, 106
Office for Standards in Education (Ofsted) 54–55, 98
Olssen, M. 106
Office for National Statistics (ONS) 99
Oxford 91, 101
Özsoy, S. 69

Pakistan(i) 104, 111–112
parents 2, 6, 24, 29, 40–41, 43, 45, 47–48, 50, 54–56, 59–60, 68–69, 86, 90, 116
Parrish, J. 18
pedagogy 8–9, 38–39, 41, 71, 82, 108–110, 112–113
pension 80
PEPS-Economie Students' Association 18

Perryman, J. 52
Peters, R.S. 4
Pietropolli Charmet, G. 45
Piussi, A.M. 38, 41
policy: educational policy 7–8, 42, 51–54, 60, 116; government policy 51, 101; neoliberal policy 50–52, 54, 60; policy-makers(ing) 52, 57, 71; social policy 7; state policy 6
politics 6–7, 92, 94, 117–118
polytechnics 93–94
population 27, 40, 53, 86, 90, 95, 101
Post-Crash Economics Society 16
postmodern(ity) 9, 41, 93, 95, 101
Powell, W.W. 6
Prassl, J. 78–80
Pratt-Adams, S. 24
precariat: precariat and schooling 81–83; precariat and the gig economy 79
Prime Minister (PM) 25, 100
Pring, R. 55
privatisation 50, 52, 54, 61, 86–87, 118
productivity 15, 42–43, 57, 64–66, 69, 72–73, 82, 84
Psychology 13, 32
pupils 3, 5, 13, 17, 41–42, 44–47
public services 50, 97

qualitative 19, 43, 65
quantitative(ly) 18–19, 69

Rahnema, M. 108
rationality 7, 13, 18, 32–33, 39, 57, 64, 68, 70, 73–75
Raworth, K. 20
Read, C. 19
Readings, B. 92, 94, 96, 101
Reay, D. 54, 59, 61
relativism 37
Research England 98
Research Excellence Framework (REF) 99
resources: human resources 37, 66, 73–74; teaching resources 98
Rizvi, F. 72, 74
Robbins, L. 12
Roberts-Holmes, G. 52
Robeyns, I. 75
Roman Catholic Church 91
Roy, S. 114

Said, E.W. 105
Santos, A. 14
Savage, G. 5
school(s): School Boards 23–24; pre-school 64, 70; primary school(s) 42, 53–54; secondary school(s) 12–13, 17, 19, 51, 54, 77
Schotter, A. 12
Schultz, T.W. 65–66

Screening Hypothesis 66
self-employed 79–80
Sennett, R. 72
Sent, E.-M. 13–14, 16
shareholders 16
sick leave 80
Siegfried, J. 17
Silver, H. 94
Simon, H. 13
Smith, A. 65
social: social life 15, 84; social mobility 51, 60–61; social relations 15, 31, 67–68, 73, 78; social world(s)/social-world 29, 32, 78, 115
social sciences 13–14
Soss, J. 50, 60
Spence, M. 66
Spivak, G.C. 105
Spring, J. 70–71
staff 1, 43, 68, 70, 85, 87, 90, 93, 99
standard economic model 14
Standing, G. 79–88
Stolze, R. 17
students 1–3, 5–6, 13, 16–19, 39, 42–43, 45–46, 50, 54–55, 58–61, 70, 74, 82, 84, 86–87, 90–91, 93, 95–101, 108–109, 112, 117
Student Loans Company (SLC) 99
Students' Union 6
surveillance 52, 59
Sutton Trust 96
Svenlén, S. 18
Sweeney, M. 98

Tan, E. 66
taxpayer(s) 24, 92
Taylor, A. 32, 35
Taylor, E. 59
teachers 2–6, 8, 16–17, 31, 39–48, 50, 52–55, 60, 77, 82, 92, 100, 108, 116
Teaching Excellence Framework (TEF) 87, 98
Telegraph 15
Thatcher, M. 50, 94
Thunberg, G. 33–34
Tieleman, J. 13, 18–19
Times 98
Tims, A. 79
Toswell, M.J. 91
Tugwell, R. 13
Turner, C. 3
Tversky, A. 14

Unal, L.I. 66–67
unemployment 27, 51
United Kingdom 6, 8–9, 15, 17–18, 42–43, 50, 59, 79, 86, 88, 90, 93, 98–99
United Nations General Assembly 29
United Nations Convention on the Rights of the Child (UNCRC) 30, 32
university 9, 13, 17–18, 42, 57, 86–87, 90–101
University of Cambridge/Cambridge University 6, 18
Uzunyayla, F. 72

Van Staveren, I. 15
vice-chancellor(s) (VC) 90, 95, 99
vocational: vocational approach 55; vocational curriculum 55; vocational expertise 8; vocational skills 104, 109; vocational qualifications 55, 61
Vono de Vilhena, D. 84–85

wage(s) 12, 14–15, 65–69, 72, 79, 85
Wales 8, 23, 90, 93, 97
Walford, G. 7, 54
Ward, S. 6
Watts, J. 33
widening participation 57, 90, 95
wealth 18, 25, 51, 68, 77, 82, 99
Weber, R. 14
Weedon, C. 5
welfare 26, 47, 57, 64, 86
Wells, K. 30–31
West, A. 1, 54
West(ern) 2, 9, 31, 38, 95, 104–106, 113
Whitty, G. 4
Whitworth, A. 8
Wilkins, A. 57–58
Wilkinson, N. 13
Wolf, A. 96
Woodhall, M. 65, 73
workforce 9, 28, 64–66, 72–74, 81–82, 107
World Bank 64, 71, 75
Wright Mills, C. 2

Zelizer, V. 27, 29
Zimmermann, K.F. 81

For Product Safety Concerns and Information please contact our EU
representative GPSR@taylorandfrancis.com
Taylor & Francis Verlag GmbH, Kaufingerstraße 24, 80331 München, Germany

www.ingramcontent.com/pod-product-compliance
Lightning Source LLC
Chambersburg PA
CBHW080925300426
44115CB00018B/2944